M000106436

Being Chosen by GOD

REV. DR. CLEVELAND BROWN

ISBN 978-1-0980-9593-2 (paperback)
ISBN 978-1-0980-9595-6 (hardcover)
ISBN 978-1-0980-9594-9 (digital)

Copyright © 2021 by Rev. Dr. Cleveland Brown

All rights reserved. No part of this publication may be reproduced, distributed, or transmitted in any form or by any means, including photocopying, recording, or other electronic or mechanical methods without the prior written permission of the publisher. For permission requests, solicit the publisher via the address below.

Christian Faith Publishing, Inc.
832 Park Avenue
Meadville, PA 16335
www.christianfaithpublishing.com

Printed in the United States of America

*Ye have not chosen me, but I have chosen
you, and ordained you, that ye should go and
bring forth fruit, and that your fruit should
remain: that whatsoever ye shall ask of the
Father in my name, he may give it you.*
—John 15:16

My wife Crystal, my daughters Angela, Kristen, my
sons Cleveland, Christopher, and Kristopher
My brothers Alonza, Willie, and Clinton
Special thanks to Gertrude Smith, Tammy Smith,
and my Atty. Ran, Randolph for their support.
Then to my Pastor Dr. Franklin Frisby

Chapter 1

I would like to begin this literary journey by recalling as far back as I can remember as a little boy growing up in southeastern Virginia to bring some clarity on who I was as God's chosen before the foundations of the world and how it came to be that He would take every test and trial and turn it into multiple testimonies and how he had plans to take the absolute mess I had made of my earlier days and present me as a bona fide miracle!

I can remember that as a little boy, I was terrified of being in the dark. Whenever I would awake at night, I could see things or figures in the shadows of darkness that would attack me to the point that my mother would race to the room to rescue me and find me curled in a fetal position, screaming to the top of my lungs! It was at this time that my wonderful mother began to teach me how to pray beginning with Psalm 23, insisting that I must know it as well as I knew my name and to be able to quote it verbatim every time these night terrors occurred in my life.

Of course, my mother knew that I did not fully comprehend what reciting a passage from the Bible was going to do for the demonic attack I was suffering from, so my mother added a natural deterrent for these attacks in the middle of the night. She attached a long string to the light switch in the ceiling and ran it all the way to the head of my bedpost where I could reach it whenever I would have a nightmare. She told me, "Son, pull on this string, and the darkness will turn into light." Right then, the seed of the Word of God as my refuge was sown into the kinder years of my life, as well as another passage in Psalm 27:1 declaring, "*The Lord has become my light and my salvation.*" Little did I realize how much I would come to need those truths and more.

After this experience, I started to make it a practice to read the Bible, and it became more and more fascinating to me. Before I knew it, the *light* in the Word had set me free from the threatening darkness that brought menacing demons in my room every night, and I am not sure when I noticed that I did not need to pull on the long string anymore, but I eventually began to sleep throughout the night because there was no more anxiety, toil, or fear, "*For He gives His beloved sleep*" (Psalm 127:2).

Chapter 2

As my love for scripture grew, I was enthralled by the passages written in red, and for some reason, I understood those words a lot better than I did the other passages written in black and white. Whenever I was reading the red letters that I now realize were the words Jesus was speaking, I would invariably begin to cry. Once again, the seed of God's Word was being planted in my spirit, and it was taking root. My mother insisted that we attend Sunday school with her, as well as the morning church service and evening service if there was a meeting scheduled! We were cautioned to make sure we were listening to the preacher's message to learn something about God. For sure, she would ask us what we learned, and we had better have something to say if it was not anything but *"Jesus wept."*

There was one Sunday that was different than any other Sunday morning. I was excited about going to services. It was not a drudgery or a routine exercise but a joy to get up, get dressed, and go. On this life-changing Sunday, I heard and understood the preacher give the message on giving our lives over to God. I was eight years old at that time, and I got up from my seat and went up to the pastor and said, "I want to give my life over to God."

He asked me, "Young man, do you know who Jesus is?"

I responded, "Jesus is the Son of God, and He is our Lord and Savior."

With my public and outward expression, I was led in the proper prayer to receive Jesus Christ and was later baptized in the name of the Father, the Son, and the Holy Ghost! This marked the day, a new beginning, and I would become a moving target and a threat to the enemy's camp although I was unaware of the future mission and destiny I was set to fulfill and the perilous roads that would unwind in front of me. I am so thankful that "*He goes ahead of me, and He makes the crooked places straight and the rough places smooth*" (Isaiah 45:2).

Fast-forwarding just a little, my next foundational encounter with God happened when I was still incredibly young. I discovered that not only did I have a love for scripture, but I was carrying a marketplace or *agora* anointing, and God had given me an unusual skill and savvy for business. I would tell all the guys whom I hung around in the neighborhood that I was going to be a businessman. As I declared it with my mouth, God started to make it happen in the natural and gave me favor with a local store owner. I was fourteen years old when I started working as a bag boy in a chain of area supermarkets called BELOs.

Even though I was hired as a bagger, my desire was to know everything there was to know about the operations of the store. I went from department to department, learning the fundamentals in produce, learning how to weigh the incoming vegetables and fruit, how to price the merchandise, as well as how to prepare and properly arrange the produce on the display tables and bins. Once I had mastered this in a short period of time, I moved to the floor to learn how to price merchandise, stock and front the shelves, and observe if any new product needed to be restocked or ordered.

After one year, my zeal and eagerness to learn everything had maneuvered me full circle and back to the front of the store, only not as a bagger, but this time, I wanted to learn how to operate the cash register. One Sunday afternoon, the manager of the store came in and caught me ringing up merchandise on the cash register when I was really supposed to be bagging the merchandise. This was fine until he stopped and asked me my age. I told him I would soon be fifteen. The problem was that I was ringing up someone's merchandise that included a six-pack of beer, and I was clearly underage and not authorized to sell alcohol. In fact, the whole store could have lost their license to sell alcoholic beverages or been closed altogether for allowing a minor to sell beer. Not only was I under the legally mandated age of twenty-one to sell alcohol, but I was also working without the required work permit for those under the age of fifteen! I had a sinking feeling this was not going to end well.

As I suspected, the manager let me go that day, and the guys in the neighborhood, some who were supposed to be my friends, started laughing and joking with me. My words had come back to mock me as they mimicked me, saying, "I'm going to be a businessman!" I took it all in stride at first until one day, I saw all the guys hanging out and laughing very loud. They looked like they were having a ball, so naturally, I ran over to see what was going on, and I asked them what was the big joke and what was so funny. And one of my good friends named Jack, who seemed to be laughing the hardest, turned to me and said, "You are the joke, Cleveland the businessman. You can't even spell businessman!" "You really believe you are going to be somebody. Man, you were born poor, and you were born Black, and that is the way it is now and always will be!"

The laughter and taunting continued as I, crushed by my friend's evil statement, sadly walked away. Nevertheless, "*the Lord is near to the brokenhearted and saves the crushed in spirit*" (Psalm 34:18). Jack's laughter hurt the most because I thought of him as my friend. King David declared, "*For it was not an enemy that reproached me; then I could have borne it: neither was it he that hated me that did magnify himself against me; then I would have hid myself from him: But it was thou, a man mine equal, my guide, mine acquaintance* (Psalm 55:13).

Incredibly devastated and hurt by my friend's derogatory words, I went to my room that night and got on my knees as I had often seen my mother do whenever she was troubled. I cried out earnestly to God. I asked Him to reveal to me the truth about my life because Jack and all the other fellows' hateful words still pierced my soul like a thousand daggers!

"Lord," I cried, "Is it true what they said about my future? Is it true that You put me on this earth to be nothing but a poor Black man?" In my heart, I knew that it was not the truth, but I needed God to confirm that He had a good plan for my life, plans to prosper me and give me a favorable, successful future!

As I continued to pray to God, I was reminded of the scriptural passage in James 1:5.

I said, "Father, Your word says if I lack wisdom about anything, I can ask You for knowledge and good understanding, and You promised you would freely give it to me!"

That night, I asked God to release the wisdom I needed to become a successful businessman by the time I became thirty-five years old. I went even further in my petition and made a covenant with Him, promising to give Him all the glory. I promised to testify to anyone who would listen or wanted to know about my accomplishment in business. I promised to always share with them about the covenant agreement we made that night.

Ending my prayer, I recall telling God, "Your Son Jesus completed His work, and His earthly assignment was finished in thirty-three years. He glorified You in this. I am asking to accomplish laying a business foundation and establishing what my naysayers declared I never would get done. Let me glorify You too. In short, Lord, let me do even greater works as Jesus promised I would do… Amen."

When I got up off my knees and climbed into bed, I felt an overwhelming assurance that God had not only heard me, but He answered me and granted my request! The dream assassins from the neighborhood corner had not succeeded in destroying my hope of becoming a notable entrepreneur with their mocking and laughing. As I turned to a comfortable position and fluffed my pillow, I also realized that God had taken the hurt and embarrassment away! He had removed every dagger thrown by my so-called friends!

My heavenly Father knew He had to heal that hurt because it was designed by Satan to destroy the vision and make me fearful to ever try again. God knew I could not achieve anything with a crushed spirit because it is impossible to bear! He met me with great grace and kindness and absorbed the pain of those crushing blows I sustained that day. I found out through firsthand experience that "*the Lord is near to the brokenhearted; To those whose hearts are humble. He saves those whose spirits are crushed*" (Psalm 34:18).

Chapter 3

For promotion cometh neither from the east,
nor from the west, nor from the south. It is
God who judges: He brings one down, He
exalts another. It is God alone who judges;
he decides who will rise and who will fall.
—Psalm 75:6–7

A couple of years had passed, and my circle of friends changed after being insulted and wounded by those who should have been encouraging me and striving to do likewise. Despite what the devil tries to use people to do, God promises *"to restore health to us and to heal us of every wound"* (Jeremiah 30:17). I was wounded that day but not fatally! God took the poison right out of the daggers I had been inflicted with when I was fired from BELOs and when everyone laughed at my dream of becoming a successful businessman.

Because I held fast and believed in my dream of becoming an entrepreneur, God faithfully begins to open another *"effectual door"* for me, and as life would have it, there were *"many adversaries"* as the apostle Paul had prophesied in 1 Corinthians 16:9. Some of my acquaintances had landed jobs as cooks in a Shoney's Big Boy restaurant, and they mentioned that there was a position opened for a dishwasher. I applied for that opening and was hired immediately.

Although my job was to be a dishwasher, like always, I had an interest in all operations of the business, so I let the assistant manager know that I wanted to train in the kitchen and prep area as a cook.

God had given me favor with John, the assistant manager, who was impressed that I was never late or absent and always assisted others in other areas if they needed me. He discussed with Dave, the manager, these attributes and the possibility of moving me into another position; however, he was not in agreement with giving me the new assignment at all. I humbly and thankfully continued to work my position as a dishwasher but believed another opportunity would come along.

As fate would have it, one Friday night, business was booming, and the restaurant was unusually busy. The busboy could barely keep up and was continually bringing me loads of dishes to wash and sanitize. To help the busboy, and to keep things operating fluidly, I also took on clearing the dishes out of the bins and disposing of the trash and waste. As I did so, I observed there was a lot of money in the bins, and I confronted the busboy about taking the waitresses' tips from the table. I told him that this was stealing, and he needed to take the money back and give it to those waitresses who had earned the tips. To my surprise, both the manager and assistant manager were in the back and overheard the conversation. The waitresses had already been complaining about missing some of their tips, so the busboy was already under suspicion, and management was also checking to see if I was an accomplice!

I always relied on the teachings I received at home, never to steal and to always be honest and trustworthy. "When you follow His commandments, God will always bless you," my mother would say. That night, I became a living witness that God will do just that. The busboy was fired on the spot; and management asked me if I thought I could handle both jobs, bussing and dishwashing, and I happily said yes. I had been doing it all night on one of the busiest nights ever! I also received a raise from sixty-five cents to ninety-five cents an hour, which was no small change for a young man in my day.

I eagerly took on my new assignments, working diligently and with a spirit of excellence that was undeniable and could no longer go unnoticed and rewarded. I have learned that everybody does not have to like you, but if you have favor with God and one person empowered to bless you, that is all you need. The assistant manager

John finally was able to convince the manager that they should invest in me and teach me the ins and outs of supervising the kitchen area and the staff. I was taught and entrusted with ordering merchandise, developing the schedule for the other staff, and filling in as an assistant whenever John needed to be off.

This new assignment was met with jealousy and ridicule from the other fellows in the kitchen. They said, "John is just using you! You are nothing but an Uncle Tom put in place to do whatever will please the white man!" It was okay because God had already let me experience this type of pain and rejection in earlier experiences with dream killers, so I had become immune to the poisonous daggers that would invariably be thrown at anyone who dared to dream of something bigger than themselves or to advance in life. I told them being used or not, I was gaining invaluable knowledge that was worth my time and effort even without getting paid for the extra assignments.

My consistency and dedication paid off because it was not long after this encounter with my coworkers in the kitchen that John gave me the position of kitchen manager, and I became shift leader over the entire crew. This was truly a move of God, and His hand of favor was stamped all over it. He showed all my doubters and haters once again that "*all things are possible with Him*" (Matthew 19:26).

Chapter 4

With all the goodness God had shown forth in my life, the coming year was filled will many surprises, changes, and unexpected tragedies. I was not quite eighteen years old when I learned that my girlfriend (Lynn) was pregnant, and I knew that my next step was to marry her and try to be the best husband and father I could be. My favor continued with Assistant manager John because he made sure I got all the hours I could handle when he learned that I was about to become a father and that I was getting married soon.

When Lynn and I did get married, John invited us to their home for dinner. I realized that God had placed this man in my life at significant junctures in my life to help me. Keep in mind that this type of socializing was rare, if not nonexistent in the sixties amid great racial tension. For example, whenever I took my new bride to Shoney's for dinner where I was employed as a leadership staff, we could not eat in the dining room. We were asked by the manager, Dave, to eat in the kitchen break room with the cooks. There was no thought of offense. It was the way things were at the time.

Despite the racial times, John had given me the authority to make out the schedule for the kitchen employees and had given me the authority to also grant performance awards that consisted of extra hours of pay for those who had exceeded expectations in the tasks assigned. This strategic way of leading the crew and gaining outstanding performance from employees was recognized by the manager, and my friend John was rewarded for accomplishing so much in operating the restaurant because he had entrusted me to lead and get results.

My days of working in the restaurant business that had given me so much training and opportunity for advancement were soon to be cut short because of the impending draft and the Vietnam war. As soon as I turned eighteen, I joined the army to train as an infantry soldier with the intent of becoming a heavy equipment engineer. Two years of service was required for an enlisted soldier because of the war. However, I committed to three years to get the assignment I desired. In 1968, I enlisted in the US Army and was sent to Fort Gordon, Georgia, for basic training, and after three weeks, I was assigned to the mess hall to Assist Sergeant. Terry who had no cooking staff because they had all been deployed to Vietnam. With over seven hundred troops to feed, several trainees were selected to work KP and to help in the kitchen every week.

As the great providence of God that prepares us for things to come or future events, my commanding officers took one look at my work experience and training as a crew leader and short-order cook at Shoney's and assigned me permanently to Sergeant Terry for the balance of my eight-week assignment at Fort Gordon. I was thoroughly prepared to take on this challenge and began to work with and train the KPs. Together, we prepared wonderful dishes of food for the troops, and I was assigned leadership over the mess hall. This earned me a stripe promoting me to E-2 at the end of basic training, and I was assigned to stay on at Fort Gordon as the base cook, and three months later, I was promoted to E-3. Sergeant Terry began to train me in every aspect of operating the mess hall, and after five months, I was promoted to Specialist 4. I knew God's hand and His favor was the reason for this accelerated promotion and blessing.

About seven months later, Sergeant Terry received orders to go to Vietnam, and those who would now be in charge wanted a Specialist 5 to run the mess hall. I was upset because I had been successfully running the mess hall since I had been assigned to Fort Gordon. Terry tried to get me promoted to E5 before he was deployed, but they found out I was three months shy of the requirement for advancing to a Specialist 5, and a waiver was needed to get

17

things moving. Terry was not hopeful this could be done, but God had other plans! The commanding officer, the first sergeant, and one of the majors had extended Sergeant Terry's orders for three months later, and Terry and I began to prepare to be granted one of the five stripes that were to be given out to over a dozen other soldiers who were seeking promotion.

Ironically, I was the only one who had not been enlisted long enough! I learned that there were soldiers who had been waiting six to twelve years to earn their E-5 or regain their status after losing stripes. God continued to demonstrate His *"favor was surrounding me as a shield,"* and *"if He was for me, that was more than the whole world against me!"* For me, the number five represented great grace, which was what I received because I was one of the five who received one of those five stripes and promoted to E-5! Nevertheless, I never got the chance to take over managing the mess hall because I received orders to go to Vietnam.

As I prepared to be deployed to Vietnam, I called my twin brother, Clinton, who was drafted in March of that same year but was delayed in going there because he was completing his training as a military police. We received these orders at the same time, and there could not be two family members in the war zone at the same time. Clint convinced me to let him go over first because he was a trained MP and felt he would not be in the line of fire. In other words, he would have a greater chance of returning home alive because of his job than I might. My two older brothers, Willie and Jasper, had served and made it back, and Clint was trying to keep it that way. Hesitantly, I agreed this was the best way. Little did I foresee the trauma that would soon hit my family.

I was reassigned to Fort Gordon to await my new orders for an overseas duty post in Germany. My twin brother Clint and I had been writing to one another every week and keeping one another informed. However, a couple of weeks had gone by, and I had not received a letter from him. I started to sense that something was wrong, so frantically I called my mother to tell her how I was feeling. She tried to reassure me that everything was all right, but in her heart, she felt it too. She began to make calls to try to get information and updates. Later, we received news of our worst fears. The Red Cross had gotten in touch with my mother to tell her that Clint had been seriously wounded in a hand grenade explosion that greatly wounded his back, and they did not expect him to make it. They promised to do all that they could to transport him home and keep him alive.

I quickly obtained leave to go and be with my family to wait for my brother to be shipped back home, and I prayed he would live through the transporting journey, which was the medical staff's biggest concern. I will never forget the day I entered the hospital room and looked over at the bed at what seemed like the other half of me. There were tubes everywhere and a huge hole in Clint's back with absorbent clothes stuffed inside to control the bleeding and a container on the floor to catch the fluids and blood. Horrified, I turned and ran into the hallway, crying, so hurt I was losing my breath.

It was as though the Spirit led me into a utility closet filled with mops and brooms, but it became my prayer closet. I closed the door, and I prayed to God to save my brother. I knew God to be a covenant keeper and that He is faithful even when we are not. I promised that if he would save my twin brother, I would serve Him all of my days, and I asked God for some way to bear some of the pain I knew my brother was in. I wanted to suffer so he could live. I was so broken. He was my twin brother, and I did not want to live without him. I begged God to give him some of my strength and save his life. Once again, God came through for me. He heard my earnest and humble cry, and Clint's life was spared. He was brought home after forty-five long and traumatic days. He was impotent and had lost the use of one side of his body. I still believed that somehow his journey to recovering all that was lost was still in the Master's plan. One of the most difficult times in my life was leaving my brother to fulfill my assignment in Germany, but I knew I could trust God. His track record was tried, proven, and faithful.

I arrived in Germany and was immediately grateful that I was an NCO because of the treatment enlisted men receive overseas by other NCOs. I dutifully served my time in Germany and brought my expectant wife (Lynn) over there, and our first child was born shortly after in 1970. I remained in Germany and served one more year and began to prepare to pick up my dream and business aspirations where I had left off to serve my country. The idea of becoming a great businessman had never left me. Before I completed my tenure with the military, I completed my high school education and began to take a college business course to prepare myself for civilian life, to take care of my family, and to manifest the entrepreneurial vision! God continued to show me favor through the excellent letters of commendation and recommendations I received from the officers I served and worked under in the US Army.

Chapter 5

When I was decommissioned from the US Army, I was twenty-one years old. A great deal had already occurred in my young life that might have discouraged or distracted anyone from their youthful dream. But not so in my case! I immediately began to put plan A back into play, to become all I thought I ever wanted to be, a great businessman. In my mind, there was never a plan B, just other appointments I had to keep. Diligently, I put together my professional resume and recommendation letters and applied for leadership roles with restaurants because of the experience I had gained in the military operating the mess hall. I was certain I would be a favorable candidate for a good-paying management position. However, I was disappointed that I had not received any immediate callbacks.

Next, I tried registering with a professional company that assisted veterans in finding suitable employment. I gave them all the necessary documentation, and I was relieved to get an immediate response from them. After reviewing my resume, I was briefly interviewed over the telephone and was offered the position of kitchen manager at a well-established hotel chain in the area. I accepted the job offer over the phone, and I was told to report to work at 6:00 a.m., but it was customary for me to arrive fifteen to thirty minutes prior to starting any job.

The manager's secretary was the first point of contact that morning. She asked who I was, and I informed her that I was the newly hired kitchen manager reporting to start that day. I watched her walk into the manager's office to let him now I had arrived. However, he never came out of his office to acknowledge my presence! I decided to sit there a while. I thought, *Maybe he's tied up with something, or he is finalizing some of the job offer details.* Rationalizing with myself, I sat there until eleven. When I could finally bear the obvious, I stood up and could plainly see through the glass window into the manager's office, and he did not look very busy, but this was the secretary's excuse upon returning to her desk.

Maintaining my decorum, I told the little lady at the desk that I was going out to lunch at and that I would return in thirty minutes. At exactly eleven thirty, I came back to the front office and waited until twelve noon before I finally took a hint and simply got up and left. Although I was grossly mistreated, I did not make a scene, but I sure did feel like I was being provoked to do so. Being a Black man during the telephone interview did not seem to be a problem for that manager, but it sure became one overnight. The staff helped him to decide that there would be no Black man in charge of them, an all-white staff.

When I got back home, I called that manager around 1:00 p.m. because I could not let it rest without an explanation or even an apology! The first thing I demanded to know was what was going on and why had he agreed to hire me and given me the job as kitchen manager, then acted as if I was not present when I showed up to begin my first day on the job? Out of the blue, he started saying, "That's it right there! It is your attitude! You have got a bad attitude! There is no way you can supervise this kitchen with an attitude like that!" If it had not been so jaw-dropping ridiculous, I probably would have laughed. But it was not so funny realizing that you were being disqualified for a job you were well trained for because of the color of your skin and the consensus of the work crew to be supervised.

All I could say to that manager short of calling him a bold-faced racist and a liar was, "Sir, you liked my attitude fine during our phone interview. You liked it so much. In fact, you offered me the job after looking over my work history and experience. Any other conversation where I displayed some type of 'bad attitude' never took place because when I showed up for work, you refused to even talk to me!" I could tell that the telephone confrontation would not end favorably for me, but I would not let him go without letting him know that I knew he did not let me begin working as the new kitchen manager at that hotel because I was Black.

As soon as I said this, his reply was, "See, that is exactly what I mean! That is what I am talking about, that attitude!" And with that fabricated excuse, he rudely and abruptly hung up in my ear, and that job ended before it even started. Nevertheless, it would take more than a racist manager to deter me from following my dream and being able to take care of my family.

Chapter 6

<hr />

*Thou shalt also decree a thing, and
it shall be established unto thee; and
light will shine upon thy ways.*
—Job 22:28

The same day, I called my brother and told him what had just happened to me. He was working at a 7-Eleven convenience store at the time, and he felt certain he could get me hired there too. It was not my dream job of managing a restaurant, but I could not be picky if I were to be able to look after my wife and daughter. With that resolve, I took the position and worked there for about six months and did so well that I was promoted to an assistant manager, and in another noticeably short period of time, I was managing that store.

With what I now recognize to be a divinely orchestrated plan, I went back to college to major in business administration because a degree was required to go to the next level of promotion and increase in pay and responsibility. I worked and attended college for two years, taking as many courses as possible and learning all I could about business operations. At this point in my life, I began to recall and realized two things: one was that light would always show up and dispel some of the darkest moments I would encounter just like my mother told me, and two was that my declaration of becoming a successful business man was following me around and even leading me into opportunities that would begin to shape my destiny and give me all the experience I needed to walk in the pathway of my dream.

"Thou shalt also decree a thing, and it shall be established unto thee; and light will shine upon thy ways" (Job 22:28).

I worked managing 7-Eleven for two more years when an opportunity to manage a KFC restaurant finally opened. I wanted to work in the food service industry, and this was my chance to do so. I completed my third year of college and successfully managed that KFC restaurant for the next four years until I was to the position of training manager in which I was responsible for training and preparing other candidates to manage and operate other stores. My good reputation and rapport had greatly increased among my peers and my supervisors. The company trusted my judgement when it came to hiring staff and placement of managing staff in other stores as soon as they could operate alone. I had gained a great deal of respect and confidence from the corporate leaders in my recommendations of reputable, knowledgeable, and trustworthy candidates for hire. I felt good about this because it put me in a position to make jobs available to people whom I knew and to help them earn a fair living and take advantage of the opportunities to advance in the company.

Although our paths had gone in opposite directions after we grew up, Jack was still an acquaintance from my youth. Because of this, and maybe in the back of my mind, I wanted Jack to see that I was now the businessman he had once laughed about when we were kids. Whatever the reason, I made a grave mistake by bringing the past into my future. My mistake was to recommend Jack for employment. He had gotten into quite a bit of trouble after I left home and even caught some jail time. When his mother learned that I was back in the area and doing well, she got in touch with me and asked me if I could help her son get out of jail and on the right track. The judicial system required that he obtain and maintain full-time employment, earning above average wages as a mandate for early release and probation. This, in reality, is nearly impossible to accomplish in most cases, but God had given me favor with my bosses, and they trusted my judgment. Therefore, I was able to convince them to train Jack in the management program, and little did I know, it would soon become professional suicide for me and separation from a business that had been a great blessing to me. I had put my reputation on the line for my old friend, and I was to personally train him and make sure he became an asset to the company not a liability. I had pitched what regional managers thought was a foolish risk by suggesting that it would be beneficial for the company to not only hire a minority but someone who had been to prison and had turned their life around because of the second chance they got from their employer. I convinced them that this would be an awesome image builder and a great brand builder for the company in the community of consumers locally and nationally.

Deep down, I really wanted Jack to have a chance at a better way of living, and I wanted to be a salient part of him making that transition and transformation in life. I wanted him to become the example for others who had made bad choices but had overcome them. After much deliberation and admonishment, my regional manager and I let Jack know that this was his chance for which most would not have taken the risk. This opportunity could open many doors for home or close them and destroy the image of all involved who decided to help.

Thanking us, Jack told my managers that he was thankful to still have my friendship, and he never wanted to let us down. He went through the weeks of rigorous training and demonstrated great skill and competencies in leading in a business setting. He did so well in fact that they immediately placed him as assistant manager, but this was short lived. The old saying, "You can't teach an old dog new tricks," comes to mind here. Before two weeks of gaining the position of assistant manager was over, Jack did let us down and had stolen the weekend sales money earned over $5,000 and had taken off to God knows where!

I was shocked, disappointed, hurt, and sorely embarrassed when I learned from the regional managers that Monday what had occurred over the weekend. As I stood there in awe of the news, the past echo of Jack's laughter at my dream of being successful in business had found its way into my present day, only it was more crushing than before because I had become a businessman, had given him a chance to be one too, and he destroyed the dream for both of us in the process. It was as though his main assignment in my life was to assassinate my dreams and to prove and manifest his awful prophecy over my life when we were just boys all those years ago. What was so ironic about it all was that I knew Jack well, and I still let that enemy in.

From that point on, I became the fool who convinced a company to put their reputation in jeopardy for a common thief. Though I did not lose my job, my rapport and relationships were forever marred with management. Their new name for me was literally "the bullshitter" that could talk anyone into anything. The trust and communication with my supervisors were irreparably damaged to the point that there was no longer discussions and important business meetings where I was included. It became unbearable to even come to work and just as difficult to do my job either uninformed or intentionally misinformed. I concluded that it was time for me to leave the company and began to immediately make plans to apply for employment elsewhere.

Chapter 7

As I transitioned from one season to the next, from one seemingly bad situation to even greater things, God always provided an opened door, a way of escape, and an exceeding and abundant opportunity that was always more than I had forfeited or lost. God was always making a way for more than I could ask, think, or pray to manifest in my life. Shortly after really being blackballed and forced to leave 7-Eleven management and KFC, I applied and was accepted into a training program with Red Lobster Inc. with a great pay increase over and above what I was making with my former employers.

I was sent to Orlando, Florida, to begin an eighteen-week training intensive in which I was empowered to complete in fifteen weeks with honors! I was granted the privilege of dining with the vice president of the company and given the opportunity to return to Virginia for the in-store training and then traveled to Richmond, Virginia, to serve as an assistant to the manager there. My primary objective was to turn that store around within ninety days because of all the bad reviews and negative health inspections it had been receiving. I welcomed the challenge and saw this as an opportunity to prove my ability to lead and to become a great asset to the business.

I was superconfident in this undertaking because I believed in my ability and all the experiences I had gained through both success and through trial and error. I affirmed to myself that I was a businessman who knew the ins and outs of making a company thrive. I knew that I could cause this store to increase and show profitability because I understood through my training in policy and function, studying successful models, and stringently adhering to the operations manual that I could set things in order as I was sent to do despite the health code violation posted in that store.

Setting things in order began with the first rule of the day, making sure that the environment represented the epitome of sanitation and cleanliness in every department to bring the store up to code and to restore a good rapport with customers and regain their confidence in dining at that establishment. The turnaround of that store happened at an accelerated pace, and I was able to accomplish obtaining a good health inspection and receive great reviews from customers who recognized the store was operating under new management.

Everything was running smoothly until the next employee meeting where the staff members complained to Dan, the head manager that they were not used to doing things the way I had set them up. I could see that they were used to doing things their way, which had gotten that store in the poor condition it was in before I arrived. All I had done was bring the store back into compliance with the operations manual of the company and the regulatory mandates required to legally serve food in a restaurant. That day, I learned what poor leadership looked like as Dan, the head manager, flowed with the consensus of the staff consenting to them going back to their old routines, and he gave them permission to disregard any further instructions I would give.

As he publicly took away my authority and undermined my very objective for coming to the Richmond store, it did not take long, only a few weeks, and the store was seemingly in a worse condition than before. It was as if the demonic state of laziness and disregard for operating in excellence had been driven out and had returned with and increased system or formula for failure! *"And when he has come to it, he finds the place swept and clean. Then he goes and takes seven other spirits more evil than himself, and they enter in and dwell there; and the last state of that man becomes worse that the first"* (Luke 11:24–25).

The resumption of horrible complaints and bad reviews in no time had reached the ears of the regional supervisor who had weeks prior been singing my praises to other supervisory staff. My name had gone before me and entered rooms my feet had yet to walk into.

For sure, God was giving me a praise and a fame where the enemy consistently tried to make me ashamed of my declaration of being a great businessman and to give up. This had become a pattern I did not recognize at the time, but sure enough, the enemy does come for the seed of the Word sown in your heart!

That week, I was called "on the carpet" as they say in ministry by the area supervisor. Upon entering his office, the first thing he demanded to know was, "Cleveland, what has happened? Why after turning everything around and functioning well is this store going south again?" I informed him of the meeting that had taken place prior to this downward spiral and how my authority and instructions had been stripped away by Dan, and that he had given the staff members permission to do things their way and not follow my instructions because he was ultimately the one they answered to.

I can appreciate my area supervisor because he brought Dan in the office and gave him an opportunity to correct the problem he had cultivated in the successful operations of that restaurant, but he stubbornly refused to follow suit and resigned from his position. As he did, I was given the management of that store which I happily accepted. My elation was soon to be short lived in receiving this promotion like many others before. As soon as the staff heard of the results of the meeting with the supervisor, they secretly plotted to demonstrate their refusal to work under my leadership because in their reasoning, I had gotten Dan fired.

The plot thickened later that week as the employees planned to take their revenge on that Friday night because they knew this was the busiest night for business at Red Lobster. I did not see this one coming because everything seemed to be adjusting to normal operations despite of the prior issues. From the hostess to the dishwasher, all planned to make that Friday night a living hell for me. They filled the dining area with patrons, took their orders, and placed them in the kitchen, then every member of staff on duty that night walked out, leaving me there alone with the exception of my only two black employees. One was a dishwasher and the other a busboy, neither of whom knew anything about food preparation! If it were not so sinister a scheme, I would have laughed in unbelief. I just stood there for a second in shock as I realized I had no cooks, waitresses, bartender, cashiers, or hostess and a restaurant filled with hungry customers waiting to be served their food.

Nevertheless, all was not lost as my plotters had hoped. I was able to recruit a few employees from other Red Lobster stores to come to my rescue to work in my restaurant that night. I lost a couple of tables with customers who did not want to wait but were surprisingly not disgruntled! By the grace of God, we were able to get the waiting patrons served satisfactorily. That week, I had to screen and hire forty new employees to keep the establishment running fluidly. This was a great experience for me and a perfect example of the Word that says, "*If God be for me, He is more than the entire world against me!*" "*What the enemy means for evil you will work for my good.*"

I had come to the realization that God was working for me and in me because of my own words, and those words were following me and manifesting around me in everything that I touched. I continued to successfully work for the company for about two more years when an opportunity to go into business for myself came along. This excited me because this was the dream! This was the goal and vision all along, to become a great businessman! All the other rabbit trails were training grounds filled with highs and lows, wins and losses, joys and disappointments. I was beginning to learn that this is all a part of the journey forward, and I had two options, to give up or keep going. I decided to boldly keep going!

Like King David, I began to *encourage myself in the Lord* and rehearse past victories. I did not hesitate in uncertainty as I made my decision to do what I had never done before. I reminded myself that I had gained valuable training and experience from management to supervisory level exposures at 7-Eleven and Red Lobster, and because of that, I should be sure-footed in venturing forth. I felt sure it was my time to go for it. It was time to manifest the dream. It was time not to build another man's dream but to establish my own. That very week, I went in to meet with the regional supervisor of Red Lobster. Their objective was to convince me to stay on with the company and be promoted to supervisor within a few months. This was their plan because they had invested a great deal in training me for leadership and had not been disappointed.

As I sat there listening to their offers to pay me a top dollar salary with bonuses and benefits, they said, "Look, Cleveland, you are already in business. This is what you have been doing all the time with no risks or overhead! That is the best of both worlds, right?"

As they relentlessly continued to try and sway me into changing my mind, the promise of the realization of "the dream" was greater. I felt that while I was still young, motivated, and zealous to pursue an untrodden path, it was time. I told them that I had to take this opportunity because it may never come around again. With that as my final decision and firm handshakes, I left Red Lobster and headed in the direction of the dream plan, hoping never to have to look back with regret.

Chapter 8

Partnership and all that can accompany that in business was one aspect of the dream of which I had not considered the ramifications. At this point, nothing mattered except realizing the dream of being a great businessman. If coming into partnership with others to make it happen was to be a part of the journey, then so be it. I realized that this partnership would be a formal agreement by two or more parties to manage and operate a business and share its financial gains. There are several types of partnership arrangements and just what type we were I did not stop to think about. I do not think I had quite learned the lesson and value of revealing your dreams and vison to the right people who are involved to help and not to dream assassins sent to hinder.

The once-in-a-lifetime offer came in the form of a formal agreement with my older brother and Leonard Parson and Ron Muse, who were associates of my brother's. They had purchased a building in downtown Newport News, and they wanted me to open and manage a convenience store. The deal was that I would have ownership along with them if I left my job with Red Lobster and came onboard with them to handle the operational aspects. So where I offered no capital, I offered myself as human capital filled with the wealth of knowledge and experience necessary to operate a business successfully that they did not possess.

Leonard Parson, the one who had invested the most cash into the purchase of the building, had agreed to my partnership as an equal owner. I did not learn until after I had resigned my position at

Red Lobster that all investors did not agree with Leonard to make me an owner as well. When I confronted him about this, he let me know that he could not make the decision for all the partners involved. My next move was to see what it would take to become an owner in this franchise. After all, this was the dream, this was the primary reason for me leaving a thriving career that offered continued opportunities to advance and one in which I was favored and had established a great work history and rapport with the company.

I learned that all the other three guys had invested $15,000 totaling $45,000 startup capital. Because I had no money upfront to invest and I was leaving a good job that paid me $27,000, I negotiated with them to take only $12,000 for my first year's salary and the difference I would forfeit to represent my part as an equal investment. We all verbally concurred, and I began work the following day. It did not take long for this deal to fall through as excited as I was about becoming part owner. Due to their poor spending and decision-making in renovating the building, I was left without money to purchase equipment or to stock the shelves with merchandise, let alone working capital to operate the store and to pay myself and employees a salary.

Despair began to set in as I began to quickly realize that the deal was going sour. It was not even two weeks later that I was calling my supervisors at Red Lobster in desperation to ask for my position back. I explained to them that the money needed to start the business had fallen through, and opening my own business was not going to happen just yet. It had not taken long for my supervisor to determine that hiring me back at that time would be a perpetual risk because of my ambition to establish my own operation. They felt that I would only leave again after a few months. They advised me to take a year off to pursue my dream and, if I was still interested a year later, to come and see them.

After that telephone conversation to try and go back to my old position, I realized that that door was closed, and I was stuck with the vision. I was quickly learning that a dream comes to pass with much hard work, setbacks, disappointments, and a conscious resolve to have no plan B. The original plan must work when you are left with no other options. That evening, I prayed and asked God to show me what to do. I knew I lacked wisdom, and He would give me what I needed to know if I asked for it. I humbled myself and began to pray. Some would say when all else fails, pray, but I would soon learn that prayer needed to be my first order of business. I climbed into bed that night, trying not to waver in my faith that God would give me the knowledge and ability to rise above this setback. He would honor the words that I had faithfully declared as an adolescent, "I am going to be a great businessman!" I thought I had plans, but God's plan was greater, and He desired to see me live out my dream far more than I.

The next day, I resolved to take the $15,000 and make the dream happen. I was determined that one of the two was coming to pass in my life. I started by making all the decisions and negotiations that pertained to the work of the contractors that would be needed to complete the remodeling. I allotted $5,000 to this and used the $10,000 to buy equipment and merchandise to stock the shelves. Of course, I had to find used equipment like freezers, shelves, and refrigerators. God met my every need by making me aware of a restaurant that had gone out of business nearby. I went to see the owner and offered him $5,000 for everything in the building, which was valued at far more, but he needed everything moved out by 4:00 p.m. that day.

He said, "If you can get it all out today, you have got a deal!"

Overjoyed and encouraged at how God was moving, I immediately rented a U-Haul truck, grabbed two guys I knew, and headed back over to the restaurant. We removed everything except the paint on the walls! There was merchandise, shelves, coolers, refrigerators, freezers, tables, chairs, and hood ranges. I had acquired everything I needed to open my store in a matter of hours except the cash registers, and I found those as well at another place who sold me two of them and gave me six months to pay for them! When I could not see a way the night before, God made a way. He had already *gone ahead of me and made the crooked places straight and the rough place smooth!* I had more than enough equipment to operate my store, to put some in storage, and to auction off what I did not need raising an additional $20,000. *God will do exceedingly and abundantly above all you can ask or think according to the power that is at work in you.* And for sure, His plan and my dream were alive and at work in me! When I thought I would give up, He would not let it be!

With the overflow of finances, I was able to order more merchandise and hire three employees. By the end of the first year in operation, we had grossed over $500,000! Ron Muse who owned the building talked with me about opening a restaurant in the building right next to us. We already had tables and chairs and other needed equipment to set it up in storage. In agreement, we cut a hole in the wall and enlarged the business, adding to it a restaurant as the second business. I was given an increased salary but still no partnership offer was presented to me after all the success I had generated. After eighteen months, we opened another restaurant, and they still refused to give me partnership in the businesses I was building! At this point, I recognized that I was being prostituted for my skill to operate and make a business thrive, but I stayed with them a little longer.

We were offered a new location to open another store, and the owner of the new plaza strip of stores wanted our business to anchor the shopping area. I applied for an SBA loan, and we received it for $90,000. It was more than enough to supply the business and to have working capital for the year. When I applied for the loan, I did so with the stipulation that I would be included as a partner. I learned that two of them were okay with that stipulation, but one other of the three partners was holding out and refusing my demand for partnership or involvement with the $90,000 loan. The SBA let them know in no uncertain terms that if their new business venture would not be operated by someone with my talent, equal experience, and success generated, they would not be granted the loan. They said I was the reason it was approved, and all bets were off if I was not to be involved as partner, and so it was. That grand opportunity fell through, and I did not find out until years later that it was my own dear brother who was refusing to be in partnership with me!

One monkey does not stop the show as they say! The SBA still offered me a loan, and I refused it at that time. All I wanted was the $15,000 they owed me and never was paid the salary they had agreed upon for my first year. Little did I know that my brother was the one refusing to pay my agreed-upon wages. I finally quit dealing with them altogether. I could see that somebody did not want me to succeed but wanted me to work like a Hebrew slave to ensure their success! Lesson learned. I decided to never do that again, but I was not about to quit on my dream!

I now know that when God decides to be your partner or you make Him your partner, you will not need any other partners. This is what our covenant was about, Him partnering with me to make me a successful businessman before I reached the age of thirty-five! God did not want those three men to share in glory in the success He was going to bring me into, neither had He made any agreement with them. He made the covenant with me, and everyone would have to declare, "To God be the Glory!"

I went to see the owner of the new plaza of shopping stores that had recently been built, and I asked him about leasing the building he had offered to the other three partners. He agreed and I went back to the SBA and applied for $20,000. I also found someone to lease me the needed equipment to open my own store. With much success, I was able to open six more convenience stores and establish my own distributing company. This was all accomplished by God, my Silent Partner, who guaranteed I would have His favor and favor with men, His wisdom, and His protection. Many doors opened for me to have continued success. It seemed that the more merchandise I purchased, the more bargaining power on the price of my products was obtained. God showed me how to use that bargaining power to sell my merchandise lower that other chain stores and, thus, generating more patrons and sales.

Armed with God's wisdom and strategies, my decision to establish my own distribution company and to buy directly from the manufacturer had eliminated the middleman. I looked for a distributor that would sell products at 6 percent or less over the manufacturer's price to enable me to apply more cash flow to my bottom line. As a result, I was able to compete with two of the largest chain stores in the area called *The Tiny Giant* and *7-Eleven*.

I had found a distributor who had recently assumed the ownership of his deceased father. The company was in Ashland, Virginia, located about 110 miles away, but the distance did not seem to matter to either one of us. We were both young, eager, and ambitious. Our zeal and aggression were turned toward succeeding in business in the Hampton Roads area. I agreed with him to obtain at least one hundred accounts that would purchase an average of $2,000 a week from him if he agreed to sell the merchandise at 6 percent or less over the manufacturer's price. After he had consulted with his accountant and uncle about my offer, they agreed to the deal. Once I settled this deal with them on the price, I negotiated a deal with my distribution center, the United Distributor Company, for generating this kind of business to receive 1 percent of all the sales to go to my company. They agreed, and this is how the United Distributors Company was birthed.

Feeling accomplished, I travelled back to Hampton Roads and hired a sales person to go to all of the mom-and-pop stores and ask them to become customers of our distribution company promising the better prices than they were getting from their current suppliers. I brought equality to the table among buyers because whether you purchased $500 or $5,000 worth of products, everyone paid the same price set above the manufacture's prices. I was able to bring on board one hundred independent stores who made me their buyer and helped me become the second largest chain of stores in Hampton Roads. I made the same deal with other vendors like Pepsi Cola, Coca-Cola, various potato chip companies, and milk and ice cream companies so that they would sell to our chain at a lower cost and offer us rebates and discounts as well to market their merchandise in our stores.

As the cash flow began to greatly increase, I was able to invest into other business ventures. I became involved in promoting concerts and soon purchased 51 percent of Three E's Productions. We began to bring the top performers into Hampton Roads venues to include Kool and the Gang, Luther Vandross, and the Gap Band to name a few. They were extraordinarily successful and were popular acts that generated big time money. I believe that this is *where the ax head fell* so to speak. This is where the change happened because it seemed that the more successful I became in this arena, the further I got away from God.

I had left Red Lobster at the age of twenty-eight and joined the Quality Store at thirty and finally went into business for myself. By the time I was thirty-four, I owned seven convenience stores, a distributing company, and a music and entertainment company. My bargain with God was to make me a successful businessman by the time I turned thirty-five. God had honored his part of our covenant agreement, but I had failed to do so. The praise and accolades of men had gone to my head that everything I touched turned to gold, and I was a young, self-made businessman. I was being glorified, praised, and became the center of attention, not God!

Chapter 9

But remember the Lord your God, for it
is he who gives you the ability to produce
wealth, and so confirms his covenant, which
he swore to your ancestors, as it is today.
—Deuteronomy 8:18

It did not take long before the enemy set the trap of the pride of life and the deceitfulness of riches for me. I had become very boastful, bigheaded, and oh so proud of *my* accomplishments. I was supposed to be boasting in the Lord and what *He* had accomplished *through me*. I had become arrogant and acted as if I did not need anyone. I can recall God sending a prominently wealthy investor by to see me at one of my locations, and I would not even go out to speak with him but insisted that he come in and talk to me. In my mind, they needed to connect with me, not the other way around!

Humility was not a strong suit for me now. I had become very foolish and neglected to give God any credit for my success. As a result, the protective hedge I had always experienced around me and the businesses He had inspired me to build was lifted. I was left open to the ravages and manipulations of satanic orchestrations that left me vulnerable to thieves and liars who only caused a downward spiral in my life. So many had taken advantage of the gifts and talents God gave me to do business and became independently wealthy. For example, the owner of the distribution in Ashland sold his business because of the success he was having in Hampton Roads, partnering with my distribution company. He began to do what he had watched me do, hiring his own salesperson to scout the area and obtain a major contract with my *Tiny Giant* competitors! In doing so, he had turned the barely thriving company around and took advantage of using my strategies against me. Before I knew anything, he had sold the company and left the country! He had made a monumental profit by selling out to a larger company who refused to honor the agreement he had with my distribution company. God had left me to my *gods* to see if any of them had the power to deliver me as He had shown repeatedly.

There were many accounts too numerous to expound upon and somehow irrelevant to my conclusion. I was warned that "*a great and effectual door was opened to me, and there were many adversaries.*" Among those adversaries were so-called friends, family members, would-be partners, and the like. Much like a roller coaster, there was a rise and fall and yet another rise. Nevertheless, God is still present in our highs and lows, in our mountaintop, and valley excursions. Once I realized my falling away, I rededicated my life to God and began to glorify Him for keeping his promise to me and helping me to fulfill purpose in the earth.

The enemy came in and robbed me of everything God helped me to build over the years, introducing me to yet another *god*, a cocaine addiction. Once the god called cocaine destroyed and stripped me of my businesses, my wife and children, my home, and my family. All I chased after in those destructive four years was to get high. I was totally out of control, yet God was still not without mercy, neither was He through with Cleveland Brown and His plan for me to glorify and honor Him before men.

He loved me through a beautiful woman, who would later become my wife. Crystal could look right through all my failures and see my potential. She showed me the love of God and stayed with me as bad as things were! She was my encourager and willed me to fight and never give up but to get up no matter how many times I had to fall. "*For though the righteous fall seven times, they will rise again*" (Proverbs 14:16). I recognize that to ever ascend, the fall is necessary. If we did not fall, we could not go to higher heights. Although she suffered much, Crystal loved me through it all, giving me hope and changing my entire life. I was determined to fight now for the ones who loved me, could see no fault, and refused to leave me. All my life, I desired this kind of love and to have the opportunity to return that love, and it shows up at the weakest, most desperate time of my life. I almost lost that love through one last attempt of the devil. *"When the devil had finished every temptation, he [temporarily] left Him until a more opportune time"* (Luke 4:13).

I could never repay God for His great faithfulness toward me, even when I was anything but faithful. He blessed me to get back on my feet and to be able to go back into business, opening yet another store. As I was on my way back up, I had a relapse and fell to the enemy's offer to use drugs again. To say that I broke Crystal's heart would be an understatement. She trusted me with that heart, put it completely in my hands, and I crushed it! She left me and took our daughter, Kristen, and that crushed me.

I became so angry because I was allowing a substance drive what was most precious to me away. I was losing the best thing that had ever happened to me. The devil taunted and kicked me at my lowest point, reminding me how I had lost one family to drugs and was about to lose another one. He tried to convince me that I would be a junky for the balance of my life and that Crystal would never come back to me, and I believed his lies. Feeling hopeless one night, I took an overdose of drugs, trying to end my life and escape the pain and the laughter of the enemy. There was my loving God again who intervened this time using my twin brother Clinton. Clinton had sensed something wrong as twins often do about one another. He came to my apartment and could not get me to answer the door no matter how hard he banged on it. When he, with much effort, got through the door, I had collapsed and was barely breathing. My brother as a man of God knew how to lay hands on me and rebuke death off me! He prayed life over me until life was restored to me. He convinced me to get help, and the following day, I checked into a rehab center where I spent the next thirty-three days in their treatment program. I will never forget that because it was my daughter Kristen's first birthday, and I was not with her.

That day, I knew I had had enough. I meant business with God, and He knew it. I had more focus than I had ever experienced. I realized and believed that if He could restore and preserve my life, He could do the same with my family. I vowed to get my family back together and never subject them to this again, and that is exactly what I did as soon as I was released and had satisfied the requirements of the rehabilitation program. I did not realize at the time that my journey, my pain, my losses, my fall, these were all precursors to the bigger plan of God for my life, to bring about the deliverance for others, to advocate for and set captives free, "*and to save much people alive…*"

Chapter 10

(Part 2?)
There Is No Love in the Heart of the city

There is no fear in love, but perfect love drives out fear because fear
has to do with punishment. The one who fears is not made perfect
in love.

We love because He first loved us.

If anyone says, "I love God," yet hates his brother, he is a liar.
For anyone who does not love his brother, whom he has seen, cannot
love God, whom he has not seen.

And he has given us this command: "Whoever loves God must
also love his brother" (1 John 4:18–21).

> A new command I give you: love one
> another. As I have loved you, so you must love
> one another. By this, everyone will know that
> you are my disciples. (John 13:34–35)

I have written two accounts of my story, combining two books,
There Is No Love in the Heart of the city and *Being Chosen by God*.
Although I have given the events of the two books and the things
that occurred, perhaps I let out the most salient information that will
greatly demonstrate God's love no matter how many mistakes we
make and His desire to work miracles in our lives when there seems
to be no way out. I want to share a few miraculous testimonies in

which I know that only God could have made these events possible, and after reading them, you will know it too.

1. God delivered my twin brother Clinton from death and destruction during his tour in Vietnam. He returned to the states only half alive and given a slim chance of survival but God! As he began to make him miraculously recover, the medical staff surmised that he would never live a normal life as the impact from a grenade had placed a large hole in his back and side. God completely restored is body and mobility, then raised him up to pastor His flock for the last thirty years!

2. I was delivered from the hands of death from a drug overdose as my brother Clinton, and Reverend Boone laid hands on me and declared, *"You will not die, but live and declare the works of the Lord!"* As they prayed, life came back into my body. When I could feel my life leaving my body after taking the overdose, God told me to call my twin brother and tell him that I loved him. This is what prompted him to come over because that call troubled him, though it was not unusual for us to say I love you to one another. When he arrived, I had passed out on the floor and would have died there if God had not given him the strength to get that door opened.

3. God used my struggle with addiction to advocate for others and to open a rehabilitation center that helped many, including a young man named Brad Keske whose life was totally transformed after his divine encounter. The first day that I met him, I led him to the Lord, and I told him that God was going to deliver him out of all his troubles. When I made this declaration, it was a prophetic decree because I had no earthly knowledge of the trouble he had gotten into. He was facing fifteen years in prison and five more years for another offence. I witnessed God grant him two miracles. The first one was in traffic court from the night of his arrest. He tried to flee the police, gaining a reckless driving charge, destroying city property, speeding, and assaulting a police officer. The day that he went before the judge, the police officers gave their accounts of the violations,

and the judge asked who I was because I was sitting next to Brad. I was not an attorney, but I believed I had something better that would help Brad. I told him that I was the president of a drug rehabilitation program and that I could help him. I let them know that all that had occurred with that young man the night he was arrested was drug related, and if he assigned him to me for six months, I could help and be a viable part of his intervention. The judge did just that despite everyone's objections and anger that wanted to see him go to prison. The second miracle witnessed was the great disciple and helper Brad became to me and the organization. Sarcastically, his court-appointed lawyer advised him to bring a toothbrush and toilet items because he was going to jail! I rebuked the words she tried to release into Brad's circumstances.

When we went to the circuit court that morning, she wanted to take Brad into the prosecutor's office to accept a plea bargain and not to listen to me because he was about to get twenty years if he did not follow her counsel. I renounced her words, and I told her I believed what God had already spoken in her office, and He would do what He had promised.

I said, "Let us just pray about it and asked God to do everything He said He would do." As we prayed in the name of Jesus, I could tell she was uncomfortable. She became terribly angry when the prosecutor who before wanted to throw the book at Brad would not accept a deal. The judge heard the case and the prosecutor's recommendation. The judge asked if I had anything to add, and I informed him of the tremendous help Brad had been to me and to the ministry since he released him to me and that I needed him. This was all that I said because I believed God heard us the first time we prayed. *"And it shall come to pass that before you call Me, I will answer you, and while you are yet speaking, I will hear"* (Isaiah 65:24). I remembered this passage of scripture, *"I am your Judge, I am your Law giver, and I am your King, and I will save you"* (Isaiah 22:22), and from the covenant of protection, *"When he calls out to Me, I will answer him; I will be with him in trouble. I will deliver and honor him"* (Psalm 91:15). I knew and had experienced the power of prayers prayed in faith, and my arsenal was loaded with weapons to refute to desires of the devil for Brad. The miracle resulted in the judge sentencing Brad to five years, suspending them to five years' probation time, and released him into my custody, making me his probation officer! Appalled, the prosecutor tried to object to the judge's ruling, and the judge silenced him, letting him know that he was in control in that courtroom, and his decision will stand. Brad's attorney confessed to me after the hearing that she was Jewish and did not believe in Jesus Christ, but after I prayed in the name of Jesus and had that kind of miracle, she was going back to talk to her rabbi about Jesus!

4. God was not willing to let go of my childhood friend/nemesis, and I discovered that by the love of God, I was not willing either. I was determined to reach Jack and bring him into the acceptance and knowledge of Jesus Christ. I knew because of my own experiences that this is the only way a man or woman can ever really know who they are and walk in the good plan God intended for them. A sincere, surrendered connection had to be made with the God of the turnaround. The Lord says, "*For I know the plans I have for you declares the Lord. Plans to prosper you and not to harm you, plans to give you hope and a future*" (Jeremiah 29:11).

It seems that from our youth up until we were grown men, we kept intersecting with each other's lives, and God was constantly using me to help him and to show mercy toward him even though he had shown himself to be a hateful critique and ungrateful user and a diehard thief. Nevertheless, each time I encountered Jack, I found it increasingly easier to show compassion toward him because I had wandered like a vagabond too, frequently flirting with death and destructive behaviors. I also realized that I had been freely forgiven of so much. Now I would, for the rest of my life, pay it forward.

Matthew 10:8 expresses my resolve in this manner, "*Heal the sick, cleanse the lepers, raise the dead, cast out demons. Freely you have received, freely give.*" This would become the substratum of my born-again witness and a foundational principle to teach those God would send to us how to leave a vicious cycle of sin and condemnation and begin to live a blessed life in Christ. I knew that everything God had done in my life was to be used to glorify Him, especially when I freely offered it back in the form of whatever I could do for others and testify of the Lord's goodness and His ability to save us from the uttermost to the gutter most! This was now the third time I would go after change in Jack's life. I watched him one day from the reha-bilitation center, standing on the nearby corner, selling merchandise he had stolen. I was compelled to go outside and approach him again that day, but little did I know that this time, his life would be forever changed.

I asked him, "*Why are you continuing on this path that can only lead to more trouble or, even worst, the loss of your life and soul?*" I explained that I understood the life of lasciviousness, a fast-moving, never-ending ride where you cannot find the breaks or the strength to stop. I asked him to come inside the sanctuary area of the center with me. He reluctantly did so but was intent on keeping an eye on his stolen goods because he did not want anybody to walk up and steal the things he had stolen! This was a hurtful thing to watch, and I knew the devil had perpetuated all these things in Jack life, and he needed to be delivered from the enemy's clutches once and for all. I remember taking him by the hands and began to pray first, calling attention to the stolen items and asking for forgiveness. I cried out to the Lord on my brother's behalf, and as I did, I could sense shackles and chains of sin beginning to break as he lost all focus on that cor-ner and his stolen good and began to cried out to God himself and receive the best goods that were brought and paid for with blood, and which was freely given. Jack caught on fire for the Lord that day. Today, he is a minister of fire and has been witnessing and preaching the gospel ever since. Often, he can be found ministering about the mercy, grace, and the love of God on that very same corner.

5. God demonstrated the miraculous and the power of His love when an elderly white man named Mr. Hormel came into my store to purchase a drink. Every time he would come in,

he would get in an argument with somebody. He was always disgruntled. God can instruct you to do some things that you would rather not if you did not revere God and desire to please him. That day, the Lord instructed me to go over and give that man a hug and tell him that I loved him, and God did too. The closer I came to him, the more his demeanor changed. He went from ranting and bickering to a very calm and peaceful state and no longer seemed mad with the world. The next day, he came to the store as he always did, but this time, I did not know he was even inside the building. He was so quiet! As he stood by the counter, I asked how I could help him, what could I get for him, and he said, "I only came for my hug."

This became a routine of his, and if I was not working that day, the next time he saw me, he reminded me that I now owed him two hugs. The only thing that was wrong with Hormel was that he was a lonely old man. His children had placed him in an assisted living facility and left him there with no visitation. We became friends after our encounter that day in the store. I invited him to Thanksgiving dinner, and he met my wife and children who showered him with even more love and acceptance. Not too long after this, I missed seeing Hormel come to the store several times, so I began to inquire around the neighborhood. I learned that Hormel was an extremely sick man and was, in fact, dying from his ailments. He had suffered several heart attacks, and the doctors said his body was shutting down, giving him only a 3 percent chance of living to see another day. I understood the facts but had learned in all my getting comprehension that the truth—of God's Word that is—will supernaturally override any facts or information. The Bible declares that, "*His Word is life; it is medicine and health to all our flesh*" (Proverbs 4:22). I prayed along these lines with Hormel and visited him daily, reading to him from the Holy Scriptures. I lead Hormel to the Lord, and he accepted Jesus Christ as his Lord and Savior. The doctors commented on how it was amazing that he was still holding on after such a negative prognosis, but the Spirit had revealed to me the reason why.

One day, I brought my wife and children in to see Hormel, thinking that we all would like to be together again and see one another before he died. As I was praying, I got a sharp, almost unbearable pain in my side. The Spirit of God told me to lay hands on him in the same place on his body and to declare that Hormel would not die but live and totally recover! I knew not to hesitate or get in the way of what God wanted to accomplish through me despite what the medical profession had decided. They only know in part, but the God who created the body knows all, and in a climate of faith, He will heal all!

My wife asked, "Did you see how Hormel's eyes brightened up with hope? He really believed you. Why did you tell him that knowing that the doctors have done all that they can and have given him only 3 percent hope of getting better?"

Often, our faith and obedience to what God tells us to do will be misunderstood, but the Word says His hope is not as the world's toss a coin in the wishing well type. His hope does not disappoint, but it is based on two immutable things, God's promise and His oath to fulfill every promise He has made. Her main concern was what if it does not happen, but that would be on God. I told her I was just the messenger of prayer and the vessel through which he spoke His desire for Hormel to live!

The very next day, Hormel was up and out of bed. Every tube had been removed, and he was sitting up in his chair, waiting for me to come visit. He said he needed to confess something to me because I was his friend, his minister, and now his brother.

He said, "Cleveland, I have never liked Black people. I had a hatred for them no matter who they were, and I believed I was superior to them. 'These people are here to be workhorses' is what I truly felt. But look at God using the love and ministry of a Black man to deliver me from both natural and spiritual death." This confession and change of heart about race and his former prejudices brought us even closer, and he wanted to be visited and supported our church. What a miraculous transformation!

6. Our miracle-working God continued to show His power as I practiced strict commitment and obedience to the things He would command me to do. Having no prior experience on what to do, God told me to hold a tent revival. I was to design and distribute flyers, announcing that there was coming a mighty miracle-working service of deliverances, healings, prophetic utterances and decrees, and anything else God wanted to do for His people. My former pastor, who never seemed to have anything positive to say about what I was doing, saw one of the flyers and insisted on knowing who told me or gave me the permission to do this and just who was I trying to mimic.

My response was, "God. I am just following and obeying God."

With that, I continued to work diligently to pull all the logistics together and prepare the area for a great meeting. We had an awesome band on our itinerary, an outstanding vocalist and group singers, area choirs, as well as an organist. They all volunteered their time and talent to this great cause. People came from all over to support the work, to hear the preached word, to praise and worship God in song, and to participate incorporate prayer for the city, interceding on each other's behalf and their individual families. For three nights, God instructed me to arrive at the site early and begin to prayer walk around that tent that God would bless the tent revival, do exploits, signs, wonders, and miracles, healing, and loose the captives, and God was faithful to do just that! It was phenomenal! We witnessed people arising and walking who had been bound to wheelchairs and walking on crutches and people declaring their healing of whatever maladies they had arrived with. The healing of the soul took place as more than thirty people came forth and wanted to pray the prayer of salvation to surrender their hearts to the Lord. One memorable occasion was when a young man named Bobby Heckstall hobbled up to the front with his walker, desiring to be healed and to be restored of strength in his limbs. He had accepted Jesus as his Lord and Savior, but the Lord pressed upon me to ask him if he realized that Jesus was also his healer.

I asked, "Do you believe God will heal you?"

He replied, "Yes."

I asked him again, "Do you believe God will heal you tonight?"

He shouted, "Yes!" and he moved his walker to the side of him.

I told him to walk in the name of the Lord Jesus. Everyone watched closely as he began to take one step without the walker, then slowly, another step, and another, until by the fourth step, he took off running around the tent as though he would never stop! When he finally stopped running, he came back to the front and grabbed the microphone to testify. He let the applauding people know that God told him if he would go to the tent meeting, he would be healed. He testified that he had seen people on television receive healing and had placed his hands on the TV screen as the televangelist had instructed but never had he felt the power of God hit his limbs and cause him to move as though he had never been debilitated. As he was talking, he was still picking his feet up and down as I had instructed him to do when he courageously took his first step without the assistance of a walker. He told the crowd that he was so glad for the tent meeting and that he had obeyed the voice of God and attended. God did just what he had promised!

7. The power of obedience to God's instructions continued to be manifested in my life and ministry as I began to form what we called "Jericho marches" throughout the city of Norfolk to pull down the strongholds of drugs and mayhem and murder. We marched and prayed to take back the territory that the devil had invaded and began to see a noticeable decline in the drug-related activity in the areas we had marched in to reclaim it and mark it as righteous, holy ground barring the enemy from those areas. We saw the power of God begin to take those territories back because of our diligent marches and prayers.

8. News of the success of the Jericho Marches being held in our city traveled quickly to other cities in Hampton Roads. A pastor in Newport News had read about one event in the newspaper and called the Norfolk city manager to request permission to hold a tent meeting with a stage and gospel entertainment. The city manager had agreed to allow this with the stipulation that he call

me and my group to go out with him to assist and participate in the meeting. That pastor never did call me because he did not want to involve me or my staff members, but the city manager called me and asked me to go out and assist them. I really did not want to do it because it was apparent that this was not what that pastor had in mind, but God insisted that I go knowing that I would obey Him no matter how I felt about it. God told me that there was going to be a hard and steady rain fall during the meeting.

He said, "When you see the rain, go out and stand in the middle of it, raise your hands high above your head and command the rain to stop, and it will stop."

When I arrived, the meeting was not going so well. The people were expecting a meeting like they had always experienced, one that generated love, powerful praise and worship, life-changing prayers, unforgettable deliverances, and miraculous healings! Many declared that the pastor and the people from his church were not Christians because they had not done anything to help the people who came to receive from the Lord and to witness is power at work. As the rain began to heavily pour down on the people and beat against one side and the top of the canopy of the tent, I did as God had instructed. I stood out in the rain where the people could see me, and I shouted, "In the name of Jesus, rain stop!" and as God had promised me, the rain stopped immediately!

As soon as the pastor saw this demonstration of faith, he began to talk negatively about what had just occurred as though it was a coincidence. He called me a fool for standing out there, thinking I could command the rain to stop. He told the people he did not care if the rain stopped, and the moment he uttered those words, it was as if the bottom of the sky opened and poured out every drop it contained! God would demonstrate his power at work through a willing vessel again to silence the mouth of the naysaying pastor. Once again, I stood out amid the avalanche of rain, but this time, I was not standing alone! I looked around me as many stood and joined their faith and authority with mine, and in the name of Jesus, we commanded the rain to cease. It stopped immediately. God is so awesome that to make sure there would be no more ridicule or doubt of His presence and anointing on His servants, the sun came out and began to shine brighter than I had ever seen it shine! One thing I knew and had experienced too many times was that God would be faithful to do what He promised. I knew He would use me mightily if I were obedient, and that He would *vindicate and avenge me speedily!*

> *And such as do wickedly against the covenant shall he corrupt by flatteries; but the people who do know their God shall be strong and do mighty exploits.* (Daniel 11:32)

9.   On the very night of that tent meeting where God stopped the rain because of our faith and decree, I would soon discover the major reason that God wanted me to be present at that tent meeting despite the maneuvers of the Newport News pastor to keep me out of the loop. There was a young man there who was a long-time addict that needed help. The pastor finally got out of the Lord's way and allowed me to speak and give my testimony. When I did, this young fellow came up to me and confessed that he had been on drugs for so many years, and he just wanted to be free. He said that he was so tired of that life but did not know or see the way out of being used by drug dealers. He said that he was plotting on killing his pusher, taking his money, and taking all his drugs.

I was moved with so much compassion because I knew of that kind of desperation when you cannot see a way out. I saw me not too many years ago and how my twin brother Clinton and Pastor Boone had rescued me the night I was so desperately seeking the only way out I could think of, an overdose! I wept as I laid my hands on that man's sunken shoulders, and I said, "I am not going to let that happen, son." I knew he was on the street with no place to go, so I brought him home with me that night after the meeting.

Confused, he asked, "Why are you doing this? Are you not afraid to take a stranger into your home who has just talked about killing and robbing somebody and who you know is an addict who would do anything to get high?"

I told him I was not afraid because I had been in the same predicament and had walked in his shoes. I, too, had felt like doing the same things he was planning when I was addicted to crack cocaine, but thank God, someone was there for me, and I would like to pay it forward and be there for him and others who need help and who need to see that it is possible to take your life back!

When we arrived at my home, I made sure he got a good warm bathe, clean clothes, and a welcoming loving atmosphere. My wife began to prepare him a meal fit for a king in my estimation, a large steak with baked potatoes and a side salad. He sat down and had dinner with my family, and we allowed him to sleep on our sofa. The next morning, the Lord impressed upon me to allow him to make a telephone call to anyone whom he needed to in the world. The young man told me that he wanted to talk to his mother, but when he called home, his daddy answered the phone. As soon as he realized it was his son, he quickly hung up the phone.

There was clearly a lot of brokenness and unforgiveness involved in their relationship. I began to listen as the young man began to share with me that he had done a terrible thing to his dad. Because they shared the same name, he had forged his dad's name and withdrew all his savings and blew it all on drugs. He was distraught and so sorry for what he had done, but his addiction had begun to dictate his actions regardless of the consequences. He had not seen either of his parents for nearly five years.

I asked him to try and think of someone who might be able to get a message to his mom. He called her best friend, who had since moved to California. It crushed that young man to know that his mother had died. He wept bitterly. Nothing could have prepared him for that news. She told the young man that she had made a promise to his mom that she would always be there to help him. He told her where he now was and about me and how I had brought him into my home to help him. She thanked me for taking care of her godchild and wanted me to receive some money to send him to where she was. I knew that was not what he needed right then, but that her door was always open to him. I shared with her that God had placed him in my care for right now, someone who understood and could show him the way out of the vicious cycle of drug use. From that night on, he continued to stay with me, and I learned that he was a very skillful carpenter. I helped him to get a good job using his skills, and it was not too long before he could afford his own apartment. God tremendously blessed him and delivered him from all addictions. After about two years, he did leave and go to California when he established his own drug rehabilitation program, and this awesome miracle of a man began to pay it forward as he had learned from his encounter with me that night at a tent meeting in Norfolk I almost did not attend.

10. It is important for me to share this miracle from God because of my obedience to His instructions. The Lord revealed to me that I had to refrain from selling alcoholic beverages in my store. The rise of alcoholism was mounting up in Norfolk, and I was a contributor to the problem by making it so available to those who struggled with the disease. When I discussed with my wife what I believed the Lord would have me to do, she was in total agreement with me. She told me that praying for my client's deliverance and chains of addictions of any kind to be broken and then providing them with the very products in my store that had them bound was contrary and would not work.

My pastor was against stopping the sell of beer and wine in my stores because of the amount of money it generated from my giving tithes and offerings to the church and its plans to build and expand. I went to my father, who had been a deacon in the church for over fifty years what to do, and he advised me not to take beer and wine out of my store because from his view, God was not against me prospering by whatever means to live well and support my family, as well as the work of the ministry. I went to yet another leader in the church, my mother-in-law's pastor with the same inquiry, and he told me he was surprised that I had come to him seeking direction about this subject because he had not too long ago visited my store and noticed that there were at least twenty people in the line, waiting to pay for their merchandise. He noticed also that every one of them were there to purchase alcoholic beverages and were standing in line, waiting to pay for their drink of choice. He remembered thinking to himself, "This is more of an ABC store than a grocery store!"

He said, "I believe that you have already heard from God, and you have your answer." He told me that he trusted that I would obey God's voice and not man's voice.

This was truly a time of testing as I wrestled with the decision, I knew I needed to make. Two particularly important scriptures and one more encounter gave me the power and the courage to do what the Lord wanted me to do.

First Kings 18:21 says, *"How long halt ye between two opinions? If the Lord be God, follow Him; but if Baal, then follow him."* And of course, the devil will come to try to rob the Word that is sown in the soil of your heart. He knows better than we all do what can be accomplished with a Word directly from the mouth of God that is embedded in the heart of a man or woman. Those individuals will become unstoppable! Satan continued to taunt me, saying it was foolish to stop the sell of alcohol in my stores and how this will financially ruin my business, but God sent another Word to deliver me in from the valley of decision. Micah 6:8 declares, *"He (God) has shown you, O mortal, what is good. And what does the Lord require of you? To act justly and to love mercy and to walk humbly with your God."* With this dynamo of a Word resting in my spirit, the Father led me to the neighborhood to prayer walk the streets, and as I did, I ended up across the street from my store in a park where the community children played every day. There I found broken wine and beer bottles all over the park, some I saw directly under the sliding boards and swings where the children could be critically hurt.

My first move was to clean the area up before the kids showed up after school. Elder Boone and I worked diligently to make that play area safe, removing all the glass and trash that had been thrown there. As I did this, I was both convicted and convinced that these broken bottles and trash had come from my store, and I knew that I did not want to be a part of the problem anymore.

After Elder Boone and I finished cleaning the area, we noticed a drunk man laid out on the park bench with his wine bottle and beer, and we began to pray for his deliverance and that he would have no more need or desire to drink alcohol. We prayed for his salvation, and as we did, he got up and began to pour the wine and beer out on the ground! He thanked us for praying for him and threw the empty bottles in the trash can. We left that park, shouting and praising God for what we had just witnessed and thanking God for answering our prayers.

I have learned personally that the devil does not want to let you go and will always seek a more opportune time to ensnare you with the same yoke of bondage from which you have been liberated. Matthew 12:43–45 says,

> *When the unclean spirit is gone out of a man, he walketh through dry places, seeking rest, and findeth none. Then he saith, I will return into my house from whence I came out; and when he is come, he findeth it empty, swept, and garnished. Then goeth he, and taketh with himself seven other spirits more wicked than himself, and they enter in and dwell there: and the last state of that man is worse than the first. Even so shall it be also unto this wicked generation.*

The next morning at six, I opened the store, and the same man we had prayed for in the park was back in the store to purchase beer and wine. He went and got his drinks from the cooler and sat them on the counter to pay for them, and I refused to sell the alcoholic beverages to him. I told him that *whoever the Son sets free is free indeed*, reminding him of how we had prayed together on yesterday for his deliverance from drinking.

He said, "Look, either you take this money, or I am just going to take this beer and wine." I told him no, and as I did, he grabbed the wine and beer and walked out the store. I started to run after him, but God stopped me in my tracks and said, "*Cleveland, you cannot sell it to them and pray for them too.*" I could hear the echo of my wife's voice as she had conveyed that very thing from the beginning.

I decided right then to stop selling beer and wine. I put a sign in the windows at the front of the store and on the coolers that after thirty days, I would no longer sell alcohol beverages in my store. I had climbed out of that valley of decision and made a God-choice to no longer be an instrument used to harm the very people God wanted me to use me to set free! I was to be a part of making the way for their deliverance from bondage. After the thirty days were over, any alcoholic products left in the store, I poured it out. As soon as I had done this, four men came to the store to buy beer, and I told them that this store no longer sells alcoholic beverages.

I stood there resolutely and relieved to make that announcement to them. As I did, one of the men said to the other three, "Now you pay me my money right in front of Mr. Brown."

He said, "They bet me that you would not stop selling alcoholic beverages here because you loved the money that it generated and that you loved that money more than you did the people. But I told them that you were a real Christian, and you did care about people."

I stood there speechless as all the men had to pay up, one owed $100, another $50, and the other had bet $20!

As the winning man collected his money, he kept saying, "Mr. Brown, you are real, you are a real MOG!" Then he leaned over and whispered to me that he had been selling drugs and, that because of me and of my example, he would no longer sell them! He no longer wanted to hurt anyone or be a part of the destructive activities already plaguing the city streets.

I smiled inside because where I could once see no evidence of love in the heart of the city, I was beginning to see it as God continued to manifest Himself in so many other miraculous encounters too numerous to write in one volume. The man asked for prayer right there in the store, and he accepted the Lord as Savior! He said he had been watching me, and he knew there was something genuine and different about me as opposed to the people he referred to as "churchgoers" and "pulpit pimps." I smiled inside again, feeling the presence of God in that store, and remembered Matthew 5:14–16, *"You are the light of the world. A town built on a hill cannot be hidden. Neither do people light a lamp and put it under a bowl. Instead they put it on its stand, and it gives light to everyone in the house. In the same way, let your light shine before others, that they may see your good deeds and glorify your Father in heaven."*

There Is No Love in the Heart of the city

―◦◦◦―

"As a mandate, prayer must be the substratum of all that we will successfully do" (Smith), which is why I am compelled to begin writing this story, my story, with prayer.

My Lord and my God, I humbly come thanking You for allowing me to have so great a vision and to be able to look through the eyes of faith and see Your desire for the city of Norfolk, Virginia. I am blessed to have been used by You within that city, and I appreciated all that You have done in my life and will continue to do. Now, Lord, as the words are released on these pages, let *my tongue become the pen of a ready writer.* Let my story become a living epistle to be read of humanity in this dispensation, making it be evident that You are the same today, yesterday, and forevermore as each reader makes the connection between how this personal journey and the divine scriptures are interwoven to empower me to accomplish things by the same Spirit who lives and exists now and forevermore. As each word is read, grant them the same vision, wisdom, and great faith to challenge the status

61

quo and do greater works! Allow the world to see what You revealed about the city during my ten years serving in the ranks from January 1987 to June 1997. Father, let great revelation come to those with whom I have and will encounter through this book or in person, the reason for this orchestrated link and bless them tremendously. Let them know the power of love and why it is imperative that we have true agape love for our fellowman.

Now, God, I shift my focus on the task at hand, which is sharing the testimony of the life You allowed me experience and to release the knowledge I have gained through this journey of experiences. My hope is to illustrate to my audience that there is a purpose for all that we go through and endure. I have learned through Your Word that the victory is given to the one who endures and continues to stand through every trial and test designed by the devil to destroy, but by God simultaneously, to cultivate supernatural strength within our very being. Finally, Father, let us realize that we must have a working faith in this life, and to have a working faith, we must have a working love because You are the epitome of love, and You require it of us. I count this petition granted, for I have boldly approached the throne of grace and made my request known, and Your Word says that You do hear me. Therefore, I have the petitions that I have asked for. In the name of Jesus the Christ, I pray. Amen.

The best starting point for me begins with the personal testimony of my own life and how I came to experience and combat the issues that were occurring right in the heart of the city of Norfolk and how I had firsthand knowledge of it. On December 15, 1986,

I found myself in a drug rehabilitation program meeting at the Serenity Lodge on Military Highway in Chesapeake, Virginia. The city hosted this gathering of about 250 persons, bringing in those who were addicted to drugs from every surrounding city in Hampton Roads. I was one in that number suffering from a cocaine addiction for nearly four years. I had undergone some intervention at a rehab center in Portsmouth, Virginia, called Green Street.

I arrived at Serenity Lodge on December 15, 1986, and watched nonchalantly as everyone stood and gave information about their struggle with addiction and how long they had been controlled by drugs, pills, or alcohol. Many had a combination of two or more things they were in bondage to in time spans of two to forty years! These people believed that they could never expect anything beyond always being an addict and subject to destructive outcomes should they fall back under the use of drugs. In other words, once an addict, always an addict, and I think they had to repeat that statement of bondage while following up with some mantra to accept that this would never change called the serenity prayer, "*God grant me the serenity to accept the things I cannot change; courage to change the things I can; and wisdom to know the difference.*" They settled into the fact that they would *always* be dependent on whatever substance they were controlled by. Not only did they unknowingly embrace having shackles forever, but they reverenced some *golden calf* called their "higher power," which had no ability to redeem, deliver, or set free. This Higher Power could be represented by a cat, a stereo boom box, and certain music, which helped them to deny their habit control. This is the reason why for several of the attendees, it was their last chance. They had been through the program twice and this was the third round, strike three, and you were out of the program. It was amazing to me that one guy even had the audacity to call another man their "higher power," who was simply his sponsor for an AA meeting he had been attending.

I remember thinking to myself, *What kinda "higher power" is that? He has the same potential and weakness to go back to the bottle as you do! What kinda' power is that?* I thought sarcastically and frustratedly as the circle around the room began to close in on me, the new guy!

The primary thing I observed and was disturbed by was that as I listened to all the people in the room profess and consider their *higher power* as anything and everything other than God Almighty, the spirit of the Lord revealed to me why we were all remained in the state we were in. We were still addicted because we were worshipping false gods and could never really be delivered until they knew and acknowledged the truth. My deliverance came that day with the revelation God had spoken to me. I renounced in my heart all the things I had held higher than Him. As I realized what the answer to all of our issues was, I was compelled by the Holy Spirit to speak that truth. Immediately I was on my feet, declaring the truth. My very being took on a life of its own as I declared, "How in the world can you say your stereo, car, or another human being is your higher power when there is only one true higher power, and that is God Almighty who sent His Son, Jesus Christ, to save and deliver us from our destructive patterns and lifestyles!" He *is* the higher power who can and will help us today if we will acknowledge Him only. He is the one who *has the power*, and He knows how to set us free from this bondage of drug use and alcohol. "*Lean not unto your own understanding, but in all your ways acknowledge Him and He will direct your paths*" (Proverbs 3:5–6).

When I stood up, I did not realize I was going to say everything that I did. When they gave me the floor and the opportunity to speak, the Holy Spirit took over and spoke for me and through me. To be sure, I was sternly and openly rebuked by the director for saying what I said. He said that I could not make my God their God, and if someone wanted a doorknob to be their higher power, they could do so. At that time, I began to weep, as I thought and perhaps even said audibly, "I am in the wrong place!" Nearly blinded by my tears, I stumbled to the hallway and sat down. I could not stop the tears as I sat there holding my head in my hands. I do not know how long I was there before I felt a hand on my shoulder, and I heard the kindest voice from one of the counselors there.

She said, "I could not say this in the meeting, but you have truly found the higher power, God through His Son Jesus Christ. This truth will deliver you."

I left the meeting that night knowing that I had been given the answer, and an urgency came upon me to come before God to seal my own deliverance. It seemed that we could not drive fast enough to get back to Green Street, the facilities where we were lodging. I hurried to my room and dropped to my knees, and I began to simply talk to God. I asked Him to forgive me of the sins I had committed, those I knew of and those I may have forgotten or been unaware of. I confessed wrong actions toward my family, friends, and fellowman in general. I took responsibility for my own deeds, acknowledged them before a loving and forgiving God, and I sincerely repented.

In my mind, I began to survey all the events that brought me to this desperate point in my life. I realized the terrible mess I had made! I realized that God had preserved me, and His grace was on my life. I had no clue that God would use this mess as a message to deliver others soon, but I did know I no longer wanted to be controlled by drugs anymore and live in that downward spiraling existence. While I was on my knees, pleading with God to take control of my life, I did not understand that He already had! In truth, His hand had been upon me all the time! As though by some divine remote control, my mind went back to the covenant I had made with God as a younger man that if He would give me wisdom to become successful in business by the time I reached the age of thirty-five, I would tell the world that He was the reason for my success, and I would glorify Him in the earth. I promised to acknowledge that my accomplishments came as a result of my covenant and partnership with God, and I was to also testify that when you trust in the Lord, He would provide for you and make you to prosper in whatever you put before Him. *"For thus says the Lord my Redeemer, I am the Lord thy God which teaches you to profit and leads you by the way that you should go"* (Isaiah 48:17).

I have since learned that God always raises you one better. *"Now unto Him who is able to do exceedingly abundantly above all that you could ask or think according to His power that works in us"* (Ephesians 3:20). He had fulfilled the promise and honored the covenant agreement just as I was turning thirty-four years old. I had opened seven thriving convenience stores in the surrounding neighborhoods, I was blessed to build my own home valuing $150,000 dollars, I possessed several cars, owned a distributing company, as well as an entertainment company, and I was generating a cash flow of four million dollars per year! God had been faithful and honored His promise to me. However, He reminded me that I did not keep my part of the covenant with Him. I quickly prayed for forgiveness for allowing the deceitfulness of riches and worldly influences to take control of my life. I had neglected to give God the glory that was due Him for what He had accomplished *through* me. I earnestly prayed that night for God's grace, restoration, and forgiveness, and I refused to get up off my knees until He assured me that He would deliver me and take over my life. I waited before the Lord for an answer. I felt like Jacob wrestling with an angel that night as I knelt on the chilly tile floor, saying, *"Lord I won't let You go until You bless me!"* (Genesis 32:26).

When I had ran out of words and tears, it seemed as if I had been on the floor for hours with no answer. I did not understand at the time His promise that *"before you call Me, I will answer you, and while you are yet speaking, I will hear you!"* (Isaiah 65:24). Unwilling to relent, I asked God to let me hear from heaven and to speak to me in the same manner that He spoke to Abraham, Isaac, and Jacob. At that moment, God took me out of my physical body and set me in the middle of a great open space, and it was as though my vision had been enhanced to see for miles and miles! I was in awe as I surveyed the vast amount of space there was. As I stood there gazing, I began to see numbers coming toward me from the distance, and when they reached me, they entered into my mind. The numbers were forty-four, thirty-four, and twenty-four, and the same numbers came consecutively as I stood there.

Finally, I said, "God, I do not understand. Please speak to me concerning this." I asked the Lord, "What does this mean? And why am I repeatedly seeing these numbers?"

At that time, I was back in my room on the floor, and He commanded me to get up off my knees and to get my Bible and begin to read. Amazed myself at how long it had been, I told God that I had not read my Bible in over four years, as though He would not know this.

He responded, asking, "Didn't you ask Me to speak to you like I did the patriarchs before you?"

I said, "Yes, Lord."

God told me to turn to Isaiah 44 and to read. When I got to the second verse, it was as though He engraved it in my spirit and wrote it upon my heart to never forget it, "*Thus says the Lord that made you, and formed you from the womb, Who will help you. Fear not...my servant who I have chosen.*" God let me know He had never left me, I left Him, and He assured me that I was forgiven and welcomed back into the arch of protection, love, and redemption. As He did this, every need and desire I had for cigarettes, drugs, and alcohol was taken away.

Following verse 2 in Isaiah, He focused my attention on verses 6–9. He showed me that I would be a witness to the world that He was a God who keeps covenant, even the covenant I had made with Him at sixteen years old!

> *Thus, says the Lord the King of Israel, and His redeemer the Lord of hosts; I Am the First and the Last; and beside Me there is no God. and who, as I, shall call, and shall declare it, and set it in order for me, since I appointed the ancient people? And the things that are coming, and shall come, let them shew unto them. Fear ye not, neither be afraid: have not I told thee from that time, and have declared it? You are even my witness. Is there a God beside Me? Yea, there is no God; I know not any.* (Isaiah 44:6–9)

As God continued to minister to me out of the next twelve verses of Isaiah 44, He revealed to me why I must become His witness because many were worshipping false gods, and their gods had no power to deliver them for addictions or sins. The verses perfectly described the scenario that had taken place at the Serenity Lodge meeting earlier that night. Verse 9–12 of Isaiah 44 says, "*They that make a graven image are all of them vanity; and their delectable things shall not profit; and they are their own witnesses. They see not, nor know; that they may be ashamed who have formed a god, or molten a graven image that is profitable for nothing.*"

God encouraged, admonished, and charged me to let the people know the truth and how He had freed me from my own addiction to show and convince them that He is that power and that He is the only way out of the destructive path they were entangled in. Perhaps the most redeeming part of that night of renewal before the Lord was when God told me that wherever I saw Jacob's name in the next verses, to place my name there because He is personally addressing me here. "*Remember these, O Cleveland and Israel, for you are My servant. You, Cleveland, shall not be forgotten of Me. I have blotted out, as a thick cloud, your transgressions, and, as a cloud, your sins. Return unto Me, for I have redeemed you. Sing, O ye heavens, for the Lord has done it. Shout, the lower parts of the earth. Break forth into singing, ye mountains, O forest, and every tree therein, for the Lord has redeemed Cleveland, and glorified Himself in Cleveland. Thus, says the Lord, your Redeemer, and He that formed you from the womb, I am the Lord that makes all things, that stretches forth the heavens alone, that spreads abroad the earth by Myself*" (Isaiah 44:24).

In that moment, in the twinkling of an eye it seemed, He blotted out the ordinances that were against me and the shame that sought to overwhelm me. God confirmed that He, indeed, had received me, restored me, and had resumed control of my life as I had asked. Now His plan, preparing me from my mother's womb to be a great witness for Him, was back on course.

With the knowledge of my redemption, the refocusing of the vision, and a fresh, powerful anointing and zeal, I returned to the city of Norfolk with a great commission given me by God Almighty. I was born in Norfolk when it was just a county with dirt roads and large ditches on each side for drainage, and it had grown into a great city, which I had come to love with from a child. It was my pleasure to be used by God to make an impact for the kingdom in this city. As I submitted to the plan and call of God, He began to open doors for me, reveal significant issues that threatened the city pertaining to drugs, and sent me forth to be a servant and a witness to the city of Norfolk.

Ironically, I was a part of the drug problem in the city from 1983 to 1987. Cocaine had just begun to become prevalent in the early eighties, as well as the drug of choice, heroin. Of course, marijuana and many other forms of pills played their part in keeping the city under a cloud of recreational use, addiction and overdoses that too often would lead to death. Following my own conversion, I opened Brown's Convenient Store, started a church, and went into business and full-time ministry. Little did I realized that the anointing of both king and priest had been released into my life. God began to use me again in an *agora* or marketplace ministry, meeting the natural needs of the community, using business and using the church to minister to their spiritual needs.

God began to use my presence in the community, and all was going well until the day I was pulled in by Federal Agents and the DEA on drug charges of distribution and conspiracy in connection with a drug ring operating out of New York and set up in Norfolk controlling the Lindenwood neighborhood. This was truly the devil's mode of operation, to destroy my witness for the Lord and to make me ineffective in influencing others to be delivered and to be free indeed by the power and saving grace of Jesus Christ. The devil knew I was sealed unto redemption and already bought with a price. I had surely gotten away and escaped his snare, but his aim now was to prevent me or my testimony from *"saving much people alive."*

"What the enemy means for evil, God uses it for my good" (Genesis 50:20). This was the exact evil circumstance that brought me into the acquaintance of Mr. Rutherford, the head of the Commonwealth Prosecutors' Office, who would later become a part of the witness I was to become for the Lord. Rutherford's mission was to put away any and every one even remotely connected with drugs in the city. When I met him, I assured him that day that I was just an addict who had been delivered by God. I told him my name was Cleveland Brown, and as God is my God, I would never be found using cocaine ever again. He told me that I would do twenty years to life for any

connection to that drug operation. He had knowledge that my past usage of cocaine was extensive and in such a high quantity that he resolved that I must have been a distributor.

Rutherford stated, "If I used the quantity of drugs that they knew about me buying, I should be dead if I had actually used it for my own personal habit." This was just another testimony of how God had preserved my life and how he had protected me from myself.

Again, I pleaded for forgiveness and the mercy of the court because I was just a former user and that my use of drugs had caused me to lose everything, my businesses, my home, my wife and family, and nearly, my life. As I gave my testimony, something apparently shifted the course of the way things were going. It looked like the worst-case scenario for me, but *"when your ways please God, He will make even your enemies be a to peace with you!"* (Proverbs 16:7). *"For I the Lord am your Judge, I am your Lawgiver, and I am your King. I will save you!"* (Isaiah 33:22). Glory to God! Finally, the head of the DEA decided to give me amnesty if I would become a state witness and testify to purchasing drugs from Chester B. Because of my meeting with Rutherford that day and the fact that I was once an addict, he felt certain I would shortly be before him again. From his perspective, once an addict, always an addict.

He stated, "A man with a $2,000-a-week habit will be in trouble with the law again."

I reaffirmed and stated again that God had delivered me. I told him that I would not be before him because of my using drugs ever again and thanked him for releasing me.

My great witness had begun at a high level, and I was to remember this event, and they would too because God intended to use it again mightily. Justice had been served that day, those who should have been gone to jail did, and the innocent was set free. January 9, 1987 has become a significant and an unforgettable date for several reasons. I was delivered out of the snare of the devil and received amnesty, I had successfully completed my tenure in Rehabilitation, and my grandson, DeAngelo, was born. Because of the love of God, the highest power, I was free and alive to celebrate and rejoice in it all!

The next three years, God kept me grounded and active through the work of the ministry and business. I felt led to plan and coordinate a parade for God in the city of Norfolk, commemorating the soon return of Jesus based on Matthew 24. The goal was to unite churches and bring them out of the four walls into the streets into *"the highways and hedges to compel them to come"* and to declare that Jesus is Lord! This is when I learned about the true condition of the heart of the city of Norfolk.

There were two pastors who were members of the city council and four born-again Christians, but none of them advocated or openly wanted to publicly release the protection and the state of the city over to God. I repeatedly tried to get a permit to host the rally and march for Jesus to begin at Tidewater Drive and convene at city hall to dedicate the city to God and to incite love and unity among churches, citizens, and officials to defeat the enemy who desired to overtake and destroy the city of Norfolk. To accomplish this, the permits department set up a meeting and referred me to Raymond Norman, the supervisor of Parks and Recreation to discuss holding a march for Jesus Rally at the Northside Park because the expense to take it to the streets would cost up to $5,000 per block. I did meet with Mr. Norman, but the idea of the park disturbed me to the point that I had to explain why God wanted it going down the route He had given to me. I believed that I had to fulfill God's request and not men. As a result, the march was put on hold. I believed that God would later open the door that was shut down due to cost and bring His vision to pass.

Undaunted, I began to write letters to area churches, and even my pastor requested them to pray and seek God about the parade for Jesus in the city of Norfolk. I explained the mission was to defeat the demonic forces that were trying to take over the city. I sent out letters to the pastors and deacons of the church that God had given me, and to members of the body of Christ at large. The theme of it all was based on a Word of knowledge from the Lord that *"it was now time to take a stand against drugs in our communities, cities, and states. The only way we are going to stop the problem is for you, my servants, to lead My people to Me, and I will heal them. Look around you and through-*

out this world and you can see that My Word is being fulfilled. You are indeed living in the last days, and time is short. The devil has little time left, so he was doing what he can to keep as many people as he can from the liberty of knowing Me. I hold you and your deacons and trustees who are my disciples responsible and accountable to be good Christians and to set the right examples for all believers to follow. I know many in my church have made mistakes, and I am putting them on notice to repent now! Christians must be true authentic epistles read of men, living a righteous life, and I grace them to do so, in order to save the generations to come."

This letter was not received well from several pastors who retorted, "We have been pastors for over twenty years, some thirty years, and God has not spoken to us about doing something like this, so why would He come to you, a novice at best, and give this message to you?"

I realized that this would be one for God from this point. I had done what He asked me to do. I recognized that God would have to open their eyes, but that Sauline spirit was to be present in my life moving forward because of the magnitude of the vision. This reminded me of how Saul hated David for the anointing released upon him and because of his relationship with God. *"Is not this David of whom they sang to one another in dances, saying, Saul killed his thousands, but David killed tens thousands"* (1 Samuel 29:5).

I even received great opposition from my own pastor, Saul, whom I had given a copy of my written testimony and the prophecy God had given me and why He was calling for me to organize and lead the march for Jesus campaign in Norfolk. He both opposed and insulted me, but I realized that when you have done this to me, you have also done this to my Father. I decided that I will humble myself and leave the church and every other naysayer in God's hands.

"But they that wait on the Lord, shall renew their strength, they shall mount up with wings like an eagle. They shall run and not be weary, they shall walk and not faint" (Isaiah 40:31). This passage burned in my spirit and kept me strong against the daggers being thrown and from bitterness that the enemy would try to let settle in my heart sent from those who were now my colleagues, whether they wanted

to acknowledge that or not. I would wait on the Lord to make a way. The *great and effectual door* was already opened for me by Him, "*and there are many adversaries*" (1 Corinthians 16:9).

When I became a servant of the Lord, my waking prayer became, "Lord, *order my steps*, lead me, and guide me throughout *this day that You have made. I will rejoice and be glad in it!*" I can recall a simple but profound lesson that God taught me while I was driving along the interstate. I observed a middle-aged white man on the side of the road with a flat tire. The spirit of a servant was upon me, and I was always looking for someone I could help, so I pulled over to see if I could be of assistance. The man told me he had been trying to loosen the lug nut on the tire but had not been able to get it to budge.

He said, "Thanks anyway, I will just call a wrecker."

I suggested that we both apply our strength to try and loosen it but to no avail. The man thanked me again and said he had roadside assistance, but it would take them about an hour to get there, and he was already late.

I said to him, "Let's pray," and I grabbed his hand, and I asked God to help us, and God gave me the thought to use my weight on the lug wrench as leverage. I put the wrench on the lug nut, leaned against the car, pressing down on the wrench with all my weight until every one of the stubborn lug nuts came loose, and the tire changed! I thanked God for His knowledge, and the man decided he would give me the fifty dollars he would pay roadside service for assistance. I refused the money because I knew God had shown me all I had to do, which was pray, and he would answer my prayer, and he was pleased with me being a servant to my fellow man. The man continued to insist I take the money, and I told him I was only doing what we should all be doing—helping one another. I got into my car and drove off.

I went to work at my convenient store, and when I pulled up to the store, I realized the man was pulling in right behind me, and he said, "Is this your place of business?" I told him it was, and he went inside and purchased $50.00 worth of merchandise.

He said, "You were a blessing to me, and I wanted to be a blessing to you."

This event and many others like it greatly increased my love walk, and as a result, my faith in the things of God greatly increased. The level of love for my fellowman and the desire to be a servant of God grew even more. God gave me many opportunities to serve others, and He blessed my business so much financially that I was able to open up another business, Brown's Fried Chicken in Virginia Beach, Virginia, another place where I could show others God's love.

Nick Avis was a new Christian, and he was on fire for the Lord. He became my partner, and we demonstrated to others how a Black and White man could partnership together, worship together, and witness together as it should be. When God made this connection, I knew it was to carry out His divine purpose in our lives. We were together for a reason and a season, but because of that time together and that relationship, God was able to direct me to where He wanted me to be. Nick was a member of Rock Church under the leadership of John and Ann Jimenez. I was invited by Nick, and I started going to that church. As a result, my prayer life mightily increased when I received my prayer language and heard others praying in different tongues. I learned to spend time in prayer every day for hours. Every chance I had available, I would talk with God, and as I sat in His presence, I then began to develop an ear to hear His voice!

I heard the voice of God one day when I was in my restaurant, and a customer came in to purchase some fried chicken. He told me to give her a copy of my testimony, and I obeyed. She did not live here but was from another country. She wanted to know why I had insisted that she take a copy as she was returning to England that day. I informed her that I was only doing what the Lord had instructed me to do. I trust that He will tell me why later, maybe not. I was simply carrying out His will. This obedient moment was to become one of the most salient events in my life and paramount to the course of my ministry. Still I had no idea why the Holy Spirit insisted that I release to her that testimony of myself written in the year 1987. Only God knew. I will share the significance later.

Meanwhile, I had come to the conclusion that the city of Norfolk was not ready to hear from God, and the pastors in the area churches felt that it was not their job or calling to solve the problems that existed within the city, and the devil and his imps ran stampeded and took control. At the time, my wife and I were attending Mt. Gilead Baptist Church under the leadership of their pastor. He became a hard taskmaster to me and a thorn in my side, so to speak. He was extremely critical and discouraging about everything I did or said at a very crucial time of the growth of my ministry, making my calling and election unsure. He had what I detect now as a jealous spirit that was *"as cruel as the grave."*

I began to draw the line when he went out of his way to belittle my wife and me because we were an interracial couple in a—apart from my Caucasian wife—predominantly Black congregation. This leader was also derogatory because he recognized that God had anointed me in the same manner that He did with King David, and he became my Saul! As Saul heard the accolades from the people concerning David, so had my leader heard of and perceived the potential of the vision I had been anointed to establish. *"And the women answered one another as they played, and said, Saul hath slain his thousands, and David his ten thousand"* (1 Samuel 18:7 KJVA).

After enduring as much as we possibly could, the pastor had made it unbearable for us to remain a part of that ministry. We left that church to seek another home church where we would be embraced and loved. We were literally chased away by the very shepherd who had been given the charge to care for us and watch for our souls! I was beginning to distinguish between true shepherds and hirelings, and at the same time, realizing that I never wanted to treat anyone in this fashion and call myself a leader! I knew I did not want the troubled souls of the city end up at that church and be lost forever because they vow never to trust a man or woman of God again based on this man's behavior and misuse of authority.

Despite the rejection we had encountered at that church, I realized that this was really a means of protection from God and a way to perpetuate His plan to equip me for the *"greater works than these"* that Jesus declared I would do. What was designed to break me and discourage me and force me to turn back and give up had only fueled me to go even further. I left that city, and we moved to Virginia Beach where I visited several churches before settling at the Rock

Church under the leadership of Pastors John and Ann Jimenez. God continued to prepare me and taught me so much from each pastor.

Perhaps my biggest takeaway came through the admonishing of Pastor John Jimenez who taught me the importance of seeking God daily about everything. He advocated and instilled in me the importance of a diligent prayer life that fostered loving and interceding for others, that would release divine strategies against the enemies' schemes, and that would develop a deeper relationship with God. As I reflect on this experience, my time at Rock Church was both salient and invaluable. However, I soon learned that Rock Church was not my rest but only a part of the journey.

Calvary Revival Assemblies of God lead by Pastor Stewart was my next spiritual training camp, and he became the leadership I needed to increase my understanding of what it meant to be chosen and to activate and enhance my knowledge of the gift of prophecy the Lord had imparted in my life. This was a great challenge for my new leader because the devil had done such a tremendous job in discouraging me and creating such a feeling of unworthiness. I think the most effective tactic of the devil by far is to make you doubt the vision and doubt if you were even called and chosen at all, especially in mandates that are gigantic, and that make you feel so small in comparison. But much like David, I had learned to *"encourage myself in the Lord"* through prayer and practicing God's presence as I had learned from the tutelage of the pastors at Rock Church.

When I was given the opportunity to minister from the pulpit, God gave me a message from Isaiah 34, concerning wars and rumors of wars. He prophetically revealed to me that we would go into battle with the Middle East, and it came to pass not long after this sermon when Kuwait and Iraq went into conflict. This was not the only conflict because many pastors in Norfolk had been declaring that God would not allow this war, but God told me to inform them that this will indeed occur, and that we would be victorious. Pastor Stewart acknowledged that this message from God was about the land of Idumean, where that battle would take place, and he gave me a map of the Middle East, marking this place near the border regions.

I loved and greatly valued my time under this great example of leadership because Dr. Stewart was the epitome of a man whom the Lord had raised up to shape the spiritual lives and destinies of those sent to him and who would achieve this without agenda, manipulation, or control. He was apt to teach, encourage, support, and most importantly, confirm that, yes, God had chosen me to do great things, and that He was going to mightily use me as I continued to grow in my relationship and knowledge of Him. "*But the people that do know their God shall be strong and do exploits*" (Daniel 11:32b KJV).

I was thankful, blessed, and released with the blessing from the man of God, who graciously recognized that his impartation into my life and the journey had been accomplished. There was nothing else that he was to do but restore, reaffirm, and build up what others had tried to destroy. The mission was accomplished as I said my good-byes, moving forward with even greater momentum and confidence than before.

God led me to my next assignment at the Word of Life Christian Church, pastored by Reverend Joseph Martin. He was associated with many other great men of God who were strong in the arenas of prophecy, tongues and interpretations of tongues, great faith, and flowed in the Word of knowledge. Being in the company of greater anointings and gifts impacted my life and ministry in a monumental way. I received the baptism of the Holy Spirit with the evidence of speaking in tongues under their tutelage, and my praise and worship in the spirit had such a deeper meaning. God gave me the ability to receive a word from Him for others to minister directly to the individual. This became a blessing to my ministry as I continued to reach out to the lost and those who were suffering and in bondage, in my hometown, on my watch. This continued to burden me.

The city of Norfolk mayor, the city councilmen, and the city manager all seemed to have a great love for the city but no love or major representation for many of its people, particularly the disenfranchised. They were the people's choice to govern and make decisions for Norfolk and to be of Service. However, it was clear where their primary interests were in tearing down and constructing grander buildings, uplifting themselves, and lining their own pockets. Meanwhile, the city became a focal point for many drug dealers throughout the country.

Open-air drug markets had been established in every neighborhood. Drug wars were being fought every day. Addicts were being produced on daily basic. The drug lords knew exactly how to build their clientele by getting them hooked on their product through a couple of free highs. After that, they could only keep coming back for more because the allure for that high was relentless. The demand for drugs was on the rise, and dealers from major cities had emerged in Norfolk. Pushers from New York, Philadelphia, Washington, DC, Florida, and even Jamaica had made their way to this hub. Drugs came in from all over, and everyone was fighting for territory. The sad and evil part of it all was that the youth were the ones who were the most negatively impacted because our teenagers were dying from overdoses, disease transmission, or fatal gunshot wounds. The robberies, shoplifting, and breaking and entering multiplied as addicts became desperate enough to do anything to get their next high. Both males and females prostituted themselves to get drugs. The enemy had truly taken over the city, and citizens were being lost every day because no one seemed to love enough to care about them. There was no love in the heart of the city for its people.

For the next two years, God placed a burden on my heart and a deep compassion for the people of the city of Norfolk. I observed people being destroyed every day, every month by the destructive vices the devil had intertwined into their lives. The Norfolk Police Department was finding vehicles riddled with bullets and dead bodies stuffed in the trunks of some of the cars. Many were being murdered in their homes, some of whom were innocent bystanders or children in the line of fire. I watched the news one day as shoot-outs occurred on the corner of the nearby Oakwood area, and the tears rolled down my face because love seemed nonexistent.

The value of human life was mundane and somehow flippant in importance when weighed against drug money. The evil spirit of murder had taken possession in the city and even the country. In 1989, there was a record number of ninety-one murders that year in

Norfolk alone. I can recall my children coming to me and asking why I was crying. They wanted to know if the people who died were my friends or if I knew them. I let them know that it was just sad and that it hurt me to see people destroying one another, going to prison for drug use and distribution, or being locked up for other drug-related crimes. I cried out to God again on their behalf for answers. What could I do for the people who were lost in the same shuffle I was? I was so thankful to God as I wept because I knew that He had pulled me out of that very pit. I knew if He could bring one out, surely, He wanted them all out. *It is not His will that any man should perish, but that all should come to repentance,"* and *"God is not a respecter of persons."* This was the burden I felt. *Freely you have received* grace and mercy, *now freely give* the same.

Happy New Year! It was January 1990, and my resolve was to say yes to God to whatever or wherever He would lead me. The first two months of the year, I saw much of the same murder and mayhem. The year had come in the same way it left. I remember Deacon Elder's house on the corner of East Avenue and Sewell's Point Road being set on fire with the family still inside who were renting from him. The enemy was doing all that he could to strike fear in the hearts of the people to exact money from them to pay the drug dealers debts. The city officials' remedy to this was not much better than what the crime lords were doing. Their answer to solve the issue was to destroy the homes that people were living in by tearing down low-income housing and reporting to the state that they were lowering the crime rate and getting rid of the drug users and dealers. True enough, the drug dealers and users were forced to move to another area in the city, but the people were left with no place to live! Their only solution was to demolish the low-income housing in Layfette Shores and build $300,000 homes and develop an industrial park in Robinhood Village. The city continued to destroy the residences that the poor lived in and build homes they could not afford!

Their primary concern was the image of the city and not the citizens that lived there. Driving the drug pushers and users out was not the major issue; it was becoming painfully apparent that the city wanted to drive out certain citizens, and the people who provided the funds for the city through government grants were awarded with funding to assist them in their dilemmas. The government wanted to solve the problem, not just shift it to another part of the city. Norfolk was trying to send their drug addicts to another city, not giving them affordable housing! However, the catch was this: not only had they displaced the drug addicts and pushers by sending them to another city, but they had displaced the poor as well, which caused many of them to get involved with dealing drugs to make enough money to be able to afford the better housing to purchase or rent.

The situation only escalated as the gangs began to form in a focused effort to protect the wealth they were generating. Fear seemed to have gripped the city as more and more, residents were cautious about leaving their homes, and even neighborhood churches started to convene earlier for fear of nightfall, catching them transitioning from the buildings to their vehicles. Also, many of their cars had been vandalized or stolen, and some people had suffered at the hands of ruthless robbers who caught them unaware. For sure, the devil had taken such a tight hold on the city that the people of faith began to wear badges of doubt and bowed to the control of the god of this world so much, the more that they secured their doors and windows, reinforcing them with bars of iron. Furthermore, they hired security guards to escort them as they exited the churches to make their way safely home where they bolted down for the evening amidst a city whose love had grown brutally cold.

Like an invisible alarm clock, God caused me to awake every single day around 3:00 a.m. I learned to arise and listen for His voice and to prayerfully focus on what He would have me to do that day. My words in the morning upon opening my eyes were, "Yes, Lord, what can I do?" I continued to pray in the spirit for direction. I had also learned how that this time of the morning was a critical time to begin to establish the order of the day and to uproot the tares the enemy had sown throughout the night in the neighborhood. It was the most strategic watch hour to combat the works of Satan and the perfect time to arrest demonic forces to abort their mission and to allow them to never see the light of day.

I commissioned the Day Spring, the Lord Jesus in conjunction with the Holy Spirit, to locate, shake out hidden traps and devices all over the city set to ensnare people and bring them into greater realms of fear and bondage to drug lords and their product. I prayed for the Lord to destroy every evil work, and I released the hounds of heaven against satanic forces. Sometimes, the devil would try to discourage me by suggesting that my getting up and praying daily was doing nothing, and the situation would never change for the better. I know now that when the devil does this, it is a strong indicator that prayers are working no matter what it looks like, seems like, or is like as God would soon reveal!

God's directions came to me clearly one Tuesday morning, and He instructed me to go and have a talked with my former pastor, of Mount Gilead Baptist Church. This was not a task I was eager to complete considering how this man had mistreated me. Nevertheless, I had told the Lord yes and raised the question, "What could I do for Him?" Here was my answer, like it or not! "Where you lead me Happy New Year! It was January 1990, and my resolve was to say yes to God to whatever or wherever He would lead me. The first two months of the year, I saw much of the same murder and mayhem. Lord, I will follow," was my commitment, and with my declarations in mind, I drove to Mt. Gilead Baptist Church, arriving around 6:00 a.m. As I pulled onto the parking lot, the Pastor was driving up as well. I got out of my car and walked over to him and told him that God had sent me to him this morning. He asked me for what reason had I been sent to him, and I could not firmly answer him because God had not given me those details. I was determined to obey the voice of God.

I said Pastor, "Well, maybe He wants you to pray for me." He invited me into his study and began to show me his collection of books that he had read, and he said to me, "You don't know anything. I know more about the Bible than you ever will!"

I thought to myself that nothing much had changed about this man, still tearing me down to build himself up or to make himself feel greater. I shook my head and could not wait for the closest opportunity to bid him good day and to make my escape!

It was surprising that for the next three days, God would wake me up in the same manner as before, and I would go and meet with pastor and hold general conversations. By the fourth day and visit on that Friday, I arrived just in time to see him entering the building, so I ran to catch up with him. As we walked into the church, Deacon Norman was waiting in the lobby. The Pastor made it known that for the last four days, I had been coming to meet with him, but "he does not belong to this church anymore," he said.

Finally, he just abruptly asked me, "Brown, what is it that you want?"

The only answer I could give him was that I was following the leading of the Spirit and being obedient to God's directives. As we all engaged in one another's company, the Pastor began to explain how he had been participating in waging war on drugs in the city of Norfolk, and he was a member of the drug task force. He felt the organization had not accomplished much besides hold meetings. He was concerned about Deacon Elder's home being set on fire, and nothing had been done to avenge this, and the perpetrators seemingly had gotten away with this destruction of property.

I empathized with my former pastor and concurred that "just say no to drugs" sounded good, but that slogan was no answer to the drug problem that was now raging in the city. The slogan at best was a nice suggestion but was without power to bring about permanent deliverance and total transformation in the lives of the people who were addicted to drugs and alcohol. I added that we must get directly involved. The reverend liked what I had said, "Just saying no to drugs is not the answer. We must get involved!" He called for his secretary and asked her to immediately make a banner that displayed those words. He said he would be using those very words as the theme for the coming meeting the following day.

The meeting the Pastor had planned was a gathering of Civic League members, city managers and councilmen, the chief of police, representatives from the FBI, the head of the DEA, and Clergy representatives from all of the churches in the surrounding areas in Norfolk. The primary reason for making this urgent connection was to deliberate on why the problem with drugs in the city was on the rise and to come up with viable solutions to resolve this menacing issue that had ruined the lives of so many people.

Much to my surprise, the Pastor invited me to the 11:00 a.m. meeting. I had accepted the invitation, but on the inside, I felt out of my league among such a prominent group of professionals. When I got up the morning of the meeting, the reluctancy and insecurity had not left me, so I decided not to go but to mow the lawn instead. The more I tried to busy myself around the yard and forget about attending the meeting, the more I was stirred by the Spirit to go. God witnessed to me that I must be in that meeting. I know His voice, and I had promised to obey and to go wherever He wanted me to go, even to this meeting! I relented and went inside to shower and dress. Still, my insecurity caused me to act with such procrastination and slothfulness that I arrived nearly forty-five minutes late!

Once I finally did arrive, I entered in on much deliberation that involved pointing the finger at one another and shifting the blame from one group to another. The police blamed the DEA, the DEA blamed the citizens, the citizens blamed the police, and the pastors blamed the city officials because mayor at that time, Mason Andrew, had formed an ineffective task force to wage war against drugs, but there were no activities that resulted in any success that could be seen. Some representatives declared that the drug dealers need to receive stiffer penalties for their crimes like life imprisonment or even death penalties in some cases! From their perspective, if the repercussions for peddling drugs were maximized, the reality of the hard punishment would curtail the continued illegal dealing in the city. They actually felt that drug addicts were simply undesirables with no real purpose in life and, therefore, did not need to be a part of their world!

As I sat there listening in dismay, I remembered that I used to think the same way about drug users and their addictions until I became an addict myself. I knew all too well how drugs could completely dominate a person's life, controlling every thought and action every minute of the day. Drugs acted as a consuming control mechanism that rules the mind and the body.

I said to myself, "They really have no idea what they are dealing with! No wonder they have not been able to come up with any working resolutions to this problem." These individuals could not relate to those who were plagued with the problem because they had no point of reference, neither did they have a heart to at least empathize with those who had been impacted.

One Pastor had the audacity as a clergy representative to say, "If I had my way, I would get them off the corner selling drugs by riding down there and shooting them in the kneecaps. Then I would put them all in the van, haul them off to jail, and dump them in!

After listening to the various statements, most of which revealed why nothing effective had been accomplished, God told me, "*Fear not. Do not be afraid of their faces.*" He told me that it was time for my voice to me heard. I trusted that God would speak through me, so I confidently stood up and became a part of the conversation.

I said, "It is wrong to devalue people or feel such disdain for an individual who is bound by drugs. It is so important that those who can make a difference utterly understand all that these people are up against. They are on a Ferris wheel of destruction that seems never ending and insurmountable. They have already lost all they ever had to their addictions being entangled with the lure of fast money and an insatiable high that can never match the awe of the first time it is used, though they try and try to repeat the thrill of it. This is the hook, people. At this stage of the game, it is no longer deliberate. They long too break free and recover their lives, their families, and professional careers, but the lure is too strong without the right counsel and assistance. A systematic and focused approach to breaking these chains must be applied and done so with compassion and caring. We must think of our own family members and children. Do you not suppose it could not have been one of them in trouble, or that they may meet with the same temptations in the future? I know you would want someone to care about the state that they are in. These same ones you all are ridiculing, hating, and wanting to destroy are someone else's son or daughter, brother, or sister, or even mother or father! I was one of them only three years ago! I was destitute and totally controlled by a substance and the devil until God lifted me out of that pit of darkness and sure destruction designed to end my life. In my heart, I wanted out! I did not want to continue living my life in that manner, but I could not get off the merry-go-round! I was no longer choosing it; it was now choosing me every single day of my existence! As I sat here and listened to the comments going around the room, I recognized one of the enemy's tactics, to divide and conquer so that he can utterly *steal, kill, and destroy.* Our primary objective here today must be to find real means of helping those who are powerless to help themselves, not to find ways to further destroy or end their precious lives. We are here shifting the blame around the room and losing sight of the real enemy! Only the devil would place such little value on a human being's life, but God so loved them. Therefore, He gave His Son who did not think it was robbery to die for them, for me, knowing that we would someday need that kind of love and redeeming power to bring us back up and out of the devil's snare, even the path we willingly chose! But God! He is the answer, and I am living proof of it!"

When the Spirit was done speaking through me, I was done. As I took my seat, I knew that much conviction had filled the room once light was shining on their despairing paradigms and perspectives. I could sense a shift and change of heart in several of the officials in the meeting. Councilman Connolly Philips stood and agreed that we must not continue to argue about what was already done but realize that *we were not fighting flesh and blood but spiritual powers in high places* whose sole intent was to destroy our loved ones and the city.

He further declared, "I know you do not think I should be speaking in this manner because I am a city official, and you advocate the separation of church and state, but it is clear that we are waging a spiritual war that has manifested in the natural lives of the people in the city. This is clear by the lack of focus and church leaders who have left off the power of interceding and praying not only for our city but for the deliverance of citizens who are bound!

I felt blessed to have the councilman stand and agree with my lengthy discourse, but God opened my mouth and filled it. I was not going to stifle one word that He desired to release in that room!

I could visibly see the Pastor's anger as he retorted, "Look, I am the one who called this meeting, and I do not really care what you all do!" As he walked out of the meeting and set a poor example, many others followed his poor example and attitude by leaving as well.

My neighbor, the department chair of Mount Gilead Education Department, stood and asked that the attendees refrain from exiting since there had been such a large turnout. It would be a shame to leave having accomplished nothing. Her suggestion was to select a president, vice president, and secretary and at least set the date and an agenda for the following meeting. The people consented, and some even reentered the room as we opened the floor to nominate a president.

To my surprise, an elderly woman stood up and said, "I have grandchildren on that stuff, and others are selling it. I do not want them to be locked up, die from an overdose, or be killed. They are my children, and they need help! I like what that young man said who spoke a few minutes ago. I want to nominate him."

My neighbor replied, "We have representatives here who are attorneys, councilmen, teachers, and clergy leadership. I suggest we nominate someone from those groups who are professionals and have experience with the public. One of them should be the nominee elected to move the organizations forward and make a difference. What that gentleman had to say sounded good in your ears, but that cannot be our reason for electing someone to spearhead this initiative. There are many other criteria that must be considered!"

At that moment, the spirit of the Lord spoke to me to get up and speak again, and naturally, I obeyed. I said to my neighbor, who oddly enough, had been my English teacher in Middle School, "I do not know much about running an organization or Robert's Rules of Order, but I do know God commissioned me to be at this meeting today. And furthermore, you cannot decline a nomination for me! As a matter of fact, I accept the nomination and feel free to nominate as many as you like. If I am not elected, then so be it!" I took my seat as my neighbor stood there in awe.

Directly after my statement, Trustee Willie Moore made a motion that we close on the one said name. Immediately the motion was seconded, and as everyone had the opportunity to vote, I was elected the president over the organization that day! James Pearce was voted in as my vice president, and Sharon (Stacy) was elected as the secretary. Feeling empowered by God and so glad I stopped fighting with Him about even attending the meeting, I assumed my presidential duties immediately, and guided by the Spirit, I knew to set up the next meeting and the objectives. With a great sense of accomplishment, I officiated in adjourning the meeting. After everyone had left, I sat in that room alone, realizing that God's plan had begun! I now had a job to do and had no idea what to do or how to get it done. One thing was for certain; God would continue to order my steps just as He had done early this morning when I tried to avoid this meeting and stay at home.

I met with James Pearce to discuss what direction we would take to solve the problem and the issues the city faced. James was supervisor at the shipyard and a great organizer who had worked with Operation Push. He advised we needed to get a name, mission statement, and get registered with the state. I informed him I would and seek the Lord for the mission and direction. We scheduled a meeting two weeks from the last, and one week had gone by, God still had not given me the plan, but I knew I had to wait on Him because I didn't know what to do. God woke me up 3:00 a.m. two days before the meeting, and I sat in the bed, and all of these thoughts began to come into my head, and I was amazed because I knew I had a plan, and if I remember it, all the people would be well pleased because we have a purpose. I started to lay back down to go to sleep and the spirit of the Lord told me to get up get an ink pen and paper and write God's plan down for the people. I got up began to write the message as follows:

a. Educate society about the user and dealer.
b. Prevent the next generation from using drugs.
c. Educate the addicted.
   1. Lead them to God.
   2. Help them to become a part of our good society.
   3. Help them get a hold on reality.
d. Educate the pusher about

1. his addiction (money),
2. how they are affecting the economy,
3. how they have more love for money than mankind, and
4. how to change their morale and outlook on life.

e. Get the world on the same track. God has lost so many to drugs, and it is time for a change.

f. Get all churches involved in getting the word of God to all of God's people, which will change the demand for the cocaine.

g. God's goal
    1. Build more rehabilitation facilities
    2. Lead them to God
    3. House the sick (addict and pusher)
    4. Work with total man
    5. Train them for jobs
    6. Reeducate mankind to love his neighbor

This was God's message to the people, that He would lead, direct, and protect us. God also gave me the agenda for our next meeting, name the organization, approve the mission statement, and line up of events to get the citizens involved in God's plan to heal the city. I knew God had a plan for me to be a witness, but I had no idea what a major part that He would use me in the city of Norfolk, which had no love in the heart of the city. The first event we did was the march for Jesus, you know, the parade that could not be done in the city. We were told to call it a march against drugs, but we carried the word of God and the love of God to the street. We marched from the city multipurpose building down Sewell's Point Road to Norview High School, where we held an hour rally, singing gospel songs and praying for the city. The chief of police, Chief Henson, led the parade, and God showed the people we must work together. The pastor that didn't want to have anything to do with what God had told me to do saw the chief of police leading the parade by his church, ran out of his church, jumped in right beside the chief, and began to march with us. We marched to Norview High where we had a stage set up, and we prayed, sang songs for hours, and asked God give us victory. The next message God gave me for the city was the police and community will be working together to rid our city of drugs with a warning to the parents if you have children selling drugs or using drugs, please call CADRA (community against drug-related activity) and get help for your kids before they are incarcerated. CADRA is the name of the organization God took control of, which was led, guided, and protected by Him. I had two thousand flyers made up, and I asked Chief Henson for permission to distribute them throughout the city, and he got permission from the city manager, and they approved the flyers.

The next major event we did was a prayer breakfast at the Downtown Radisson Hotel where we brought together city officials, civic league presidents and citizens to educate them about drugs, drug addiction, and drug dealers and to pray for our city. The mayor was the keynote speaker, chief of police, city manager, head of narcotics, human resource, and I were also scheduled to speak. I was nervous as I could be, and I felt not worthy to speak to such an assortment of people, and God had not given me anything to say.

The meeting was a very important one and everyone who was asked to attend came. The meeting started with prayer and breakfast. The head of narcotics was the first to speak, and he pulled out this kit with all types of drugs that were being used and sold in the city. He also had the tools used to indulge in the various types of drugs. He had marijuana, cocaine, heroin, acid, pills, and every size of package sold in the city. He had an excellent presentation to educate society. When I saw all these drugs, cocaine, and pipes, I felt the desire to use come upon me, and I had to exit the room quickly. Now I hadn't used drugs in three years. I didn't understand this effect the drug still had on me.

I stood in the hall and called out to God and asked, "Lord, how can I help the people when I can't even see drugs without wanting to use it? What if someone comes to me and give me their drugs because they want to quit, and I can't destroy them because I want to use them?"

The spirit of the Lord told me to go back in and give my testimony about all I had been through in the four years I was on drugs and the things I saw others go through and how children were being treated at drug dens. Homes taken over by dealers and used as crack houses. Mothers of children not feeding them because they were more concerned about getting high. Fathers buying pampers and later taking them back to get cash to buy drugs. Women selling themselves to buy drugs or committing all kinds of sexual favors for a hit on the pipe. How I lied to my father and mother to get cash and gave it to a dealer. How I tried and tried to quit and the control of drugs wouldn't allow me to stop. How my body responded to the color of yellow cars because the best drugs I purchased came from a dealer who drove a yellow vehicle, and when I saw a car that was yellow or even looked like his's, my body would have this uncontrollable desire to get high. I talked about how I set at a table for days, smoking crack, not even getting up to go to the bathroom, eat, or drink until my body was so dehydrated it began to cramp up all over. How I felt the only way I could quit was to overdose and die because I didn't want to be a junky anymore. When I finished speaking, God allowed me to see the compassion of everyone there because tears of hurt were coming out of the eyes of the people, and they became concerned about the people caught up in this terrible cycle. God had shown them that people needed help. God had shown me what He pulled me out of and if I didn't ever want to go back, I needed to hide myself behind Him and He would protect me forever, and that is what the people on drugs and dealers needed to know.

The Prayer Breakfast opened the heart of the city official to begin to reach out to the citizens and give CADRA the opportunity to work with every branch of the city. The city of Norfolk had a press conference brunch at the Norfolk Botanical Gardens, and George Crawley, the assistant city manager, invited me there to speak. The message was not to be afraid of the dealer in our city because we would get rid of the pushers who were causing citizens of the city to rob and steal to obtain drugs. We as a people must help our police department find the dealers. The pushers are most likely to be users or fearful persons used by the dealers to sell their drugs. The user sells it to make money to support their habit, and the dealers are businessmen working for profit. Both need help because users need rehabilitation to free them of their addiction, and dealers need jobs or business opportunities to make enough money to live up to their expensive habits of materialistic living. I explained earlier that I thought the city really wanted to help the people, and communities had to get involved and take our city back. I was speaking from my heart because the assistant city manager, George Crawley, had convinced me he was behind the vision God gave me for the city.

The press conference was successful. I received calls and also the city did as well. Citizens wanted to know what they could do to help. The city referred calls to me, and I met with community leaders to help teach them about the problem we faced. I had pastors call who were referred to me by the city, and they wanted to know what department of the city I worked for, and I told them I worked for God, and I was amazed that they couldn't work with me because they couldn't get any recognition by working with a man of God. They wanted the city to assign them a position. God showed me favor with the citizens and the city of Norfolk, but I later found out the city was using God's plan to benefit themselves and not the people. The first problem came when we were given a building in our community to house drug addicts. Assistant manager and vice mayor, had me meet with Harry Bleh, head of human resource, George Musgrove, head of human services, and Moses Jr., professor at Norfolk State University.

I poured out my heart to them about things God had shown me about the city working together. Police and citizens had been getting pushers and addicts off the streets, but they needed help with their addictions, finding places to stay, jobs and food for their families. This required every department of the city to work together to help the people. We submitted a request to change the zoning of the building to multipurpose use for the rehab that was given to us and the Planning Department approved it, but we had to go to the city council for their approval.

The meeting was set for 7:00 p.m., and I met with George Musgrove to ask him to be there on our behalf. He surprised me with a no and told me, the assistant manager was going to be at the council meeting to oppose the plan, and it would never happen. I was shocked because I was led to believe we were all looking forward to this as a way to get rid of the demand for drugs. I rushed up to the city manager's office and met with the assistant manager and found out he was totally against the plan. The police program came from this vision, and I was told when they raided neighborhoods to rid them of drugs, they would refer the addict to us.

Chief Henson had worked well with CADRA. He came to all the rallies we had in the communities and supported the ministry. I will get back to that, but let me finish what happened that night at the city council meeting. I gave my presentation, and the assistant manager spoke against it. During the time for voting, a councilman (whom I knew well, we played on the same basketball team) decided to speak to the council. He told them it would be a very bad decision to open a rehab center where the neighborhood have drug dealers, and the place didn't have a recreational area, and all I would do was to create a place for dealers to sell drugs. I was very disappointed in his speech, but I later found out that it was all just a plan to prevent us from helping the people because the city was receiving funds, and they didn't want the competition. I also found out a year later why a councilman spoke against the rehab. The reason was (my Saul) of Mount Gilead, the pastor of my church, had gone to him and asked him to kick against the drug center because I was trying to take his church. I was only being a servant of God for the people of God. I wasn't even thinking about preaching nor pastoring a church, but like Saul, he recognized the anointing.

When I left the city council meeting, I told the assistant manager that I would complete the task God gave me without his help. God gave me a greater anointing and special commission to stand in the gap and pray for the city. We started a Jericho March to tear down the wall of Satan throughout the city of Norfolk. God used just a handful of people, Vincent Boone, James Pearce, his wife and son, Reverend Amos, and myself to defeat Satan in the city. We picked several locations given to us by God and walked around them seven times for seven days. We would march early in the morning before sunrise, and we would march until the sun went down. We would pray on every corner, and we would get good reports. For example, drug dealers were misplacing drugs, hiding it from others and could not find it. Drug dealers hid drugs in attics, and water pipes would burst and wet drugs up. People overdosed and left for dead did not die! Addicts would come to us, asking for prayer, getting saved and placed in rehab. Shooting stopped during the night we marched.

While the city slept, we were battling the evil forces that had come upon the city of Norfolk. People were coming to us, taking us home with them to pray for their parents, children, and homes. The corner of Sewell's Point Road and Johnson Road was the worst in the city, and God established an outreach rehab center right in the heart of where the drug addict and dealers came from every city to sell and buy drugs. When we came out to pray, we were cursed at, told to leave by the manager of Tinee Giant because we were blocking the business, but they allowed the twenty-five to fifty people gather in front of the store every night. We rented the building next door and opened up an outreach center. The mayor had changed, and Mayor Joseph Leafe had taken over, and God used him, and he became a great supporter of CADRA. He came to the opening and dedication of the building, also cut the ribbon and offered his support.

The first day we cut the ribbon, God showed us the very reason He wanted us to be there because a young lady came in to get some help, and everyone was telling her we weren't open, and we were there only to dedicate the building, but God told me to help her. She was smelling up the place and was very high on cocaine and needed God's help. I asked her if I could pray with her, and she said yes, and as soon as I grabbed her hands, she began screaming that I was going to kill her, and she pulled away from me and began to run and hid behind a desk. I knew immediately it was a demon afraid to be cast out of her, and I told her I was there to help her, and the closer I got, the more afraid she became, and the people began to come against me because they didn't see what I saw, and they began to say I was going to cause the lady to have a heart attack, and I needed to stop, and God told me to get from among them, and He will set her free, and I calmly asked the lady to step into the back room, and she grabbed my hand and followed me. When we got into the back, I shut the door to shut them all out in order for God to do His work. The door opened, and Laura Patton came in back with me and said God sent her to assist me. I then rubbed some oil on my hand and called for God to remove this demon and these drugs from out of the woman, I asked Laura to anoint her forehead with oil in a cross, and she passed out, and I caught her and laid her gently on the floor.

God told me to open the door, and I found everyone in a circle, praying. We were all on one accord, and the young lady got up praising God and asked if she could sing a song, and she did. She sang "Amazing Grace," and her voice was shocking to everyone in the building, and they had tears of joy in their eyes, and they all knew this place was ordained for the work and vision God had given me.

Mayor Joseph Leaf gave CADRA the recognition it deserved throughout the city. He gave a banquet to honor CADRA for work we did in the city, and I was given a plaque of appreciation for the fight against drugs in the city. I thanked him and the city for honoring my Father, who is in heaven, because CADRA was led, guided, and protected by Him, and it was God's plan, not mine.

I met the owner of Tinee Giant one month after opening up the outreach, and he was glad we opened up because we cut down the drug traffic and removed addicts in front of his business, which caused his store customer count to increase, which increased his income. I mentioned to him we tried to get a 501c3 because we wanted to get some government grant, and he introduced me to a lawyer from Kaufman and Canoles by the name of Ran Randolph who was chosen by God to oversee this ministry professionally. Ran and I talked the first day, and he saw the vision clear and felt the love of God, which was needed in order to save the people. Ran and I became great friends because he was very honest, sincere, and committed to doing whatever was needed to make the ministry a success. He got the 501c3 and became the registered agent for the organization. He then incorporated his best friend, Joe Fiveash, who was also an attorney of the firm who came on board and helped put the board of directors together and researched grant opportunities for us. Ran also got us an accountant who owned his business by the name of Mack Brown who also loved the Lord and saw the vision of God for the people. They offered hours and hours of free service and fulfilled every request the ministry needed of them.

The next door God opened was at Norfolk State University, where Paula Shaw, a grant writer for the university, was employed. Paula was a member of Mt. Gilead Baptist Church, and she became a member of the board of directors, and she allowed her entire staff to work on grants, brochures, letter writing, and documentations of CADRA success. I want to remind you how I had no idea how I was going to run CADRA, but God assured me that He would provide all that was needed to help the people in the city. I was amazed at the favor God showed me and how many people were being helped and the work that was being done through prayer and being obedient to God.

The next door opened was at the College of William and Mary when Prof. David Aday came on board as one of the board of directors. Professor Aday assigned four of his students to work with CADRA and do a feasibility study of four years on CADRA to determine the effect it had on the city. God used this report to prove to the city the people needed Him. Gary King, a graduate of William and Mary, worked for the city of Norfolk and was a student of Prof. David Aday. He informed me that the assistant city manager had requested Professor Aday's service to evaluate CADRA and assess how the city could duplicate our program. Once he met with us, he found out there was no need to duplicate something that was successful, and he became one of our board of directors. God had a plan for the city, and I was extremely thankful to be a part of the master plan.

When we were looking for a place for the ministry, we focused on a large apartment building or school that we could house the addicts, train them, and provide spiritual support. We were trying to put the entire vision together in a year or two, but God had given us a twenty-year plan. I remember He had Mother Jordan from Oakwood Chapel Church called me and talked to me about opening up the CADRA center in the shopping strip where we had been planting seeds on a daily basis but had not considered that place for our rehab. When she told me the plan God gave her about using that building, I said to myself, *Why didn't I think about that?* God reassured me that it was His vision and plan. Mother Jordan had the desire to rent the building, renovate it, and purchase the furniture. I waited for this to take place, but Mother Jordan later told me it would be a while before she could carry out her plan. I didn't want to go ahead of God. I prayed about the location, and God gave me confirmation that was the site. I approached Mother Jordan with the idea of me financially putting the center together, and I didn't want to take an idea God gave her, and she said that God used her to plant the seed, and it was okay for me to finish the project. She said if He wanted her to do so, He would have provided the funds for her to do it herself. That statement she made, God would provide, was a proven fact in the days to come.

I paid the lease, building deposits, Dominion Power, and contractor to renovate the building, which caused me to decrease my inventory in my business. I put God's work first, and God increased my business in one day the same amount I spent to open up CADRA over 3,300.00 dollars. God did provide cash needed to replenish my inventory and increase my volume. God once again increased my faith and trust in Him in all that I do. Community against drug-related activities put together the first event in the city that pulled all the city departments out of the four walls and into the community. This was where they could help the people they were paid to serve. The event was set up on the corner of Johnston Road and Sewell's Point Road in a vacant lot. We put up a stage, tent, and booth for officials to work to represent their departments, social services, human services, fire department, police department, drug counselling, health department, and Virginia employment office and we had a great turnout. God wanted us to work with the total man to meet every need in order for us to heal the sick and help the lost. When God began to provide service to the people, they felt love and knew that someone cared about them. On that same corner where there was evil, our God brought good over bad. Where there was hatred, now there was love. The same area where the firefighters, rescue workers, and the police feared because of the drug wars and murderers threatening their lives, it was love. The city officials were there to aid the citizens due to the grassroots group of concerned citizens working with the police and city. PACE was born (police-assisted community enforcement).

Assistant city manager, George Crawley, pushed this idea to the community to increase property taxes to support this program that would lower the crime rate in the city. I suggested to Marty Watson that the police should get out of their car and walk among the communities to get to know the business owners and citizens they are to protect. The communities should not fear the law enforcement but learn to use them because they are paid servants who can't do their jobs without the help of the people informing them about the problem that exist in their neighborhood. Marty worked directly with Assistant Manager and was assigned to have brainstorming meetings about how to rid the city of its drug problem and reduce crime. I began to give them the ideas that God gave me, and they would use them to get the support of others to reach out the same way. Before I knew it, the rally was reconstructed by the city, other churches and community leaders. God then began to use us in a very different way.

Governor Wilder set up a meeting in Hampton that pulled together all the mayors, chief of police, city managers, human service directors, and grassroots organizational leaders of every city in Virginia to come together and find solutions to the state drug problem. I was invited to the meeting and attended, knowing I had to represent my Father God. When I arrived at that meeting, the police chaplain of Hampton was leaving because he said the people didn't want to hear what he had to say because they don't want to hear from God. I told him I was going into the meeting to represent God and share the vision for the state and the city God gave to me. The facilitator of the meeting was from Florida, and he said the meeting would not have department heads. No major, no chief of police, and no city managers because this was an open meeting; everyone had a voice, and no one was allowed to pull rank. We were broken down into groups, and we all were to take the day coming up with ideas. At the end of the day, present the best ideas and come up with the best overall solution to combat the drug problem. The group I was with all morning rejected everything I suggested about what God wanted. Not one of my ideas had been written on the board for a final vote. A statement was made that all I was talking about wasn't reality, speaking of love, and the Bible, and I knew God's plan for the people would help every city in here, and it seemed as if I had no voice in here at all. I got up and went to lunch. I was later approached by one of the facilitators and told that I had won, and I said, "Won what?" He then said as the facilitator, it was his job to make sure everyone's opinion be voted on, and they did, and three of my ideas were selected. One was that we had to prevent the next generation from getting involved with drugs. We need to get rid of the demand of drugs by building more rehab centers and put them where the demand was higher to heal the land. The third thing was the city working with churches to educate them and get their support to help solve the problem. The rest of the day before they closed a vote, they would say, "Let's see if Christians have anything to add or say."

The next week, I received a letter from the government office from a grant writer concerning supporting CADRA, and they wanted a report on what was being done by the organization. I sent them the report on the outreach center, clients we had, the number was over one thousand adults, and the youth outnumbered them. I also told them the hours we worked was whenever needed. We were available twenty-four hours, seven days a week. We had clients from all over the city. The governor's office sent a representative to visit the program to see why we were in such a demand. Jack, the representative of Governor Wilder, rode with me throughout the city. I took him to the ocean view area, where we met a fourteen-year-old girl prostitute who took us to the house she worked, and there were over eight girls living there from ages thirteen to eighteen years old. The parents of a eighteen year old were incarcerated for drug possession. The girl was not able to pay rent, so she sold her body and took in other girls who ran away from home, and one of the girl's parents was also incarcerated. Jack was amazed how I was able to connect with the girls and placed them back with their parents and receive support from social services to assist others as well. This work gave us the opportunity to receive a governor's award, which gave us a grant of $150,000.00 for two years for at risk youths. This program allowed us to begin to help the parents of the youth because many of the parents needed drug counselling and rehab. Someone to help the parents get out of jail, find jobs, and support their family. This led in to going to court with addicts who were arrested for possession or selling drugs to support their habit. The first court case was in circuit court before Judge Rutherford, the former prosecutor who was the head of the Commonwealth attorney's office a few years earlier in 1987.

I told you earlier in my book about Mr. Rutherford, and I also said you would know how God would use the event when He was prosecuting me. I told him the only reason I would be before him would be to help someone else because God delivered me from drugs. Judge Rutherford was still on that same mission to put away everyone who committed a crime to protect the citizens from the drug user and dealer. I pleaded to him for client who had fallen into a pit and was on drugs and been used by others to commit crime to pay off drug debt. I knew her mother and father well, and we had gone to school together. I asked the judge for mercy because what God had done for me, He would do for others. The judge gave her twenty years and suspended all of it providing she would commit to the program. Judge Rutherford also told her that if she listened to me and followed the plan he knew that she would never be back before him.

He also stated, "Mr. Brown could lead you to the water, but he can't make you drink, and I hope you do."

Mr. Brown has made me a believer that people can change with the help of others. The scripture of the woman at the well came in my mind as he was talking, and God told me that was a personal word for her from Him. Write the scripture here, John 4:6 verse through the 15.

> Now Jacob's well was there. Jesus, therefore,
> being wearied with His journey, sat on the well,
> and it was about the sixth hour. There cometh
> a woman of Samaria to draw water: Jesus saith
> unto her, give me to drink. For His disciples were
> gone away unto the city to buy meat. Then saith
> the woman of Samaria unto Him how is it that
> Thou being a Jew, askest drink of me, which am

a woman of Samaria? For the Jews have no deal-
ings with the Samaritans. Jesus answered and said
unto her, if thou knowest the gift of God, and
who it is that saith to thee, give me to drink; thou
wouldest have asked of Him, and He would have
given thee living water. The woman saith unto
Him, Sir, thou hast nothing to draw with, and
the well is deep: from whence then hast Thou
that living water? Art Thou greater than our
father Jacob which gave us the well, and drink
there himself, and his children, and his cattle?
Jesus answered and said unto her, whosoever
drinketh of this water shall thirst again: but who
so ever drinketh of the water that I shall give him
shall be in him a well of water springing up unto
him. Sir give me this water, that I thirst not neither come hither to draw. (John 4:6–15)

Judge Rutherford knew that CADRA was being led by God,
and we had a twelve-step program that was scripture based. All our
clients had to study the Word and go to church to hear the Word and
also become doers of the Word. He gave us client after client, and
when he became chief judge, he wrote a letter to all the other judges
to refer their clients to our program that had a desire to change.
CADRA helped the addicts by finding them jobs, places to stay, and
even transportation to work. Rev. Vincent Boone was our job coor-
dinator, and he put more people to work than Virginia Employment
Commission. God showed us favor with employers, and our clients
were very successful working and supporting their families. God continued to use CADRA to provide a help for the citizens of Norfolk.
We obtained a house across the street from CADRA where we began
to house women who were pregnant and on drugs and had no way
to support themselves or their newborns or expected children. God
placed on the heart of Laura, one of our volunteer staff, to ask a
doctor from Kings Daughters Children's Hospital to meet and work
with these mothers. We had eight babies born, and with prayer and

the doctor's advice, all were healthy. We helped the mothers find places to stay, get support from social services and churches until they were placed on a job to support themselves. God continued to provide for His people. We believed in serving one another, and God would provide what was needed. I wanted to personally thank Laura and Reverend Boone for their dedication and hard work and their obedient will of God that made the ministry so successful.

God also added Jermaine to our staff, and she became my assistant administrator and was a great help to our mission. She came on board and did all the paperwork, got tough with every client, monitored our clients, and organized our numbers to prove the work God was doing through CADRA. We placed people in rehab, and she made the referrals and made appointments with city, state, and other facilities needed to assist our clients. She was excellent in implementing assistance to our clients. She was also an addict. How great is our God!

God also used my cousin, Anthony Powell, to fill the job Jermaine had prior to her taking it over. He was great with the clients. Whatever we needed to get them to do, they really enjoyed doing what Anthony asked of them. He was also my personal prayer partner. He opened up every day and began with a prayer for the leaders, workers, and members of CADRA. God blessed Anthony with amazing abilities because he was disabled, and no one felt he had the ability to remember things or keep his balance when he walked. God used him mightily in this ministry, and Anthony was proud to serve God, his cousin, and the people of God that no one wanted to help.

CADRA was so successful in putting people to work that we obtained a contract from the social service office to put those on welfare to work. The government had given the city funds to train those on welfare for jobs to get them off assistance. CADRA put a program together to train them in three areas, computer skills taught by my wife, Crystal, carpentry taught by Brad, and managerial training taught by Cleveland. The city gave us thirty-six people and thirty-six thousand dollars, and ninety days for us to train them and get each a job. The clients they assigned to us were all dropped out of school, on drugs, and had never been employed. They gave us ones they felt had no chance of succeeding and asked us to be 100 percent. We reached the 100 percent, and everyone completed the class and were motivated to work and were very proud to be on their own to support their family. We took away every barrier that would prevent them from learning and gave them hope, love, and motivation.

The ninety days was a Trial, and upon completion, we were to get a contract from the city to handle their welfare to work program, but they decided to award it to a company out Baltimore, which was a friend of someone in the city, and they told us it was because our bid was one thousand dollars per client, and their bid was five hundred dollars per client, and they could handle one thousand clients, and our maximum was fifty. We provided daycare service, transportation, breakfast, and lunch. The company they chose was only providing classes, and they could afford to hire teachers and instructors. What we provided was one-on-one personal training and spiritual motivation. CADRA set out to help the youth that were joining gangs and selling drugs also fighting for territory. We began to meet with youth to find out what made them sell drugs and explained to them that this would put them in jail, get them killed, or get them to become addicted to drugs they sold. I became friends with them, and they began to trust me. They told me of drug wars that were about to happen.

I prayed to God, and we walked the streets to prevent them from happening. God blessed the city many nights while people were sleeping. We were walking, praying, and stopping youth from murdering each other. We couldn't stop them all, but we did the majority. The ones we couldn't stop were the most difficult to deal with. Reverend Vincent Boone's son, Diny, was shot to death while lying on a sofa at his girlfriend's house. Someone kicked the front door open and fired on him, hitting him in several places. I know my brother in Christ had talked to his son over and over about coming out of the world of drugs. He had made his mind up to get out, and Reverend Boone found him a job the same week. When he called me to come to the hospital, I went in to see all the angry people who wanted revenge and how they were his son's friends and ex-partners who couldn't understand anything but violence. Reverend Boone and I just prayed for his son. His mother asked me to go in to pray for him.

She said, "Please ask God to not let him die. God knows you. Please, Cleveland. You haven't heard anything until you hear the cry of a mother for their child's life."

I asked God to spare his life that night, but Diny died. Reverend Boone said to me he knew his son was saved because he prayed with him, and he had accepted Christ and was ready for a new beginning. Because of Diny's death, war was about to break out everywhere. I saw youth walking around with guns, thirteen years old or eighteen years, even up to thirty years of age.

Governor Wilder's office sent a letter to Rev. Vincent Boone because of his loss, and he wanted to know what he could do to help us with the youth. I told Jack, one of the governor's representatives, that we needed jobs or businesses where we could put our youth to work. When they joined these gangs, they work to control their businesses; everyone had a job to do. They are professional workers. Selling drugs is like a corporation for them.

Jack said, "If I could get them together, the governor would love to talk with them about their needs."

I explained this to Frankie J who had about fifteen workers from the ages of thirteen to twenty-five. I asked him to bring them into CADRA's office. We would get them a business to work because I had talked to the governor's office and if they quit selling drugs and explained to the government why they were involved in selling drugs, I could convince the government to support a business venture for his group. Frankie explained he always wanted to be a businessman, but Blacks couldn't own anything, and young people never would have a chance, so he was playing with the hand he was dealt. He respected me highly, and I had a great relationship with him. I remember days I came on the corner, and he would ask for prayers and would tell the guys to leave the corner and not to give me any trouble. He encouraged others to respect me. He knew that I loved him unconditionally, and God had me there for a reason to help them all.

I remember the day I called the governor's office when he came in with about ten of his workers, the youngest was thirteen years old and I called Jack at the governor's office like he asked and told him I had the guys there. I put him on speaker phone to convince the guys that I was real and serious about getting in touch with the governor. I asked Jack to talk with them. He asked several questions, and they answered him candidly and did not hold back. He was amazed I was able to have such an impact on them, and they came to this meeting. I asked him to have the governor to come to the phone just to say something to convince the young people we were trustworthy. He wouldn't support the idea, and he said to Jack that Frankie J needed to quit selling drugs or go to jail. I was shocked at his attitude. Frankie left there in disbelief, and I lost some of my credibility but not all because they knew I tried. Frankie J still had trust in me. The trust he had in me allowed him to still come to me for prayer and advice. I convinced him to go to church, and he did, and he would come back and talk to me about his experience.

One night about five-thirty, he came to talk with me, and I had an appointment with a young lady who had a court date and was out on bond. Her bondsman hadn't been paid, and he wanted her to turn herself in. I told Frankie I would be back in about an hour because I had to go downtown to take care of a problem. He said okay, and he would be back in a couple of hours. I went downtown to jail and took care of the problem and came back to the center. It was about 7:00 p.m. I waited until 9:00 p.m., and Frankie never came back. I wanted to know what was troubling him because he truly wanted to talk because he said, "I have to talk with you." I went home and went to sleep and woke up about 4:00 a.m. I went for my early walk and prayer with God.

When I heard the news that Frankie J and two others were shot to death, I fell to my knees with hurt. This thing was just before the change was about to come. We lost another to this battle that God had us fighting. I cried out to God for a reason and for Him to help me through this because I had a true burden for the people and felt I was losing. I didn't realize the thousands God had saved through His ministry. God used this to give me a message to the city of Norfolk and surrounding cities in Hampton Roads. I called it a message to the city from God. God has given me a plan for this city and the surrounding cities of Hampton Roads area. Many of us look at the drug dealers and drug users as undesirable people who shouldn't exist. But we must begin to reach out to many of these offenders, who often are children who are lost and confused, looking for a way of life. Some might feel that the three people who recently lost their lives deserved it. I look at them as young men who were lost in sin and needing the love of God to convict them. As people of God, we must begin to take back our children from the evil forces presently in high places that have hardened the heart of many youth to a point that a life means nothing. As adults, many of us have turned away from God, and there are generations that don't even believe in God Almighty. Because God has given me love for everyone, drug addicts and drug dealers respect me and accept the fact that God has placed me here for them. They came in seeking His love, plans, and help to solve their problems.

Because of the way we treat one another, we have allowed the devil to possess our youth. We stand back and talk about people, instead of correcting them by loving and guiding them and displaying proper examples for them to follow. To solve a problem, you must first know what is causing the problem. Our youth pursue the same things that we do—love, authority, leadership, a business of our own, material items, money, and power. The world of drugs offer them these things, but the consequences aren't anything that is to be desired such as being a slave to dealers and to drugs, robbery to keep up the habit, loss of morals, evil spirits that possess you to the point that you don't care and will do anything to be popular among your peers, and the most devastating of all, death.

The main problem is that people have become so selfish and self-absorbed that they have neglected their own children and other children who need their help. When Satan places that kind of attitude in person's heart, everything changes. God placed us here to serve Him and "be ye helpers one to another not ourselves."

As a husband or wife, you should look at your family's needs, as lawyer, your clients' needs, and as the mayor of a city, you should look at the citizen's needs. We need to begin to love our neighbors and help them when things go wrong. Don't talk about them and persecute them. Lend them a hand and do the righteous thing toward them. Lead them the right way because the lifestyle we live will certainly affect our children.

President Clinton said, "There is going to have to be a change to solve the problems of America," and I agree. Our society's whole attitude must change in order for God to step in and solve the problems. There have been times when funds were sent to this area for minority businesses in order to give them an opportunity to start new businesses. There are many minority candidates here who have desire, talents, and good ideas but who lacked the funds to pursue their dreams. The funds that should have been accessible never got to these people because of selfishness. The money was kept at the top for people already in business. There have been funds placed here in this area, which could support the ideas that God has given me but going to people that wouldn't help God's work. Many now work against these efforts and have attempted to model new programs after this already successful one. These are selfish people placing self-recognition and praise above the true needs of often the downtrodden. There are pastors who have gotten angry because of the way CADRA has been blessed and no longer support this mission I feel because God did not give them the vision.

God said there would have to be a change in the hearts of the people. When we focus our hearts on Him and see others through our heart, then we would treat each other better, and all our attitudes would get in order, responsive to God's word, and this city would be what God chooses it to be, a righteous city. A city in position to serve as an example for other Cities.

In my vision of CADRA Restoration House, we would love the people, reeducate the people, fill them with God's word, and God Almighty would do the rest. There would be hundreds of lost and confused people coming back to society with new vision, love, joy, peace, happiness, and right attitude. These individuals would now know how to serve and respect one another. They would have developed in them the ability and desire to work and a willingness to do the best they could to help their employers. These activities would be in their best interest because they would reap the benefit of gainful employment and be in a position to support their families. God's people in His church must now repent, change their selfish attitudes, and look toward God for His plan in their lives.

CADRA's plans are to pull together God's army to begin to do Jericho marches in every area of Tidewater cities to break down the stronghold to prepare for God's people. These multifaceted people will enter with love to aid the needy and to destroy all open-air drug markets that Satan has set up to show his force of power. They will interact with dealers and users who are trapped by evil forces to break the bondage and set them free. They will work with these ex-offenders to establish businesses so that they can be employed and support their families. This initiative is designed to open a rehabilitation center to restore the whole man. This initiative will free participants from addictions, educate former and at risk drug abusers and dealers, train participants in employment skills, assist participants in obtaining jobs, assist with shelter, assist with financial management training, provide vocational training skills, and provide counseling needed for formal reentrance into society.

I sent a package to President Clinton that included a letter, budget, brochure, and CADRA T-shirt with our mission slogan on it and asked for him to meet with us about solving the drug problem because I knew God had put him in the position to help the people get off drugs. I received a letter back that the people elected him. The next thing I knew, he was doing all he could to change the laws to lock up people for life, and with three strikes, you would not able to have parole. A person with third offense could be someone stealing a $2.00 bottle of wine can go jail for life. Minors were treated as adults, and parents were calling me to help their children who were caught with little amount of drugs, were facing five to ten years because they were addicted to drugs. I presented a package to the city and to my board of directors, and we found out through a source that there were funds that the state of Virginia was receiving from Federal Government and that had not been used, and it was going back each year.

We applied for it and were award 2.5 million, but we had to get the city to approve it and put up about two hundred thousand, which could be services amounting to that amount, and they aggrieved, and we had to go to Richmond, the capital, to meet with them to sign for the funds. City attorney, my attorney, Councilman Conley Phillip, human service manager, city manager, and I all drove up in two cars. We got there and went into the conference to discuss the plan and found out the money was part of some money the city had already used, totaling to fourteen million, and if we got the 2.5 and were successful, they would give us the opportunity to get it all. They decided not to sign for the money, and we drove back. All of them and my attorney got in one car and gave me the other car and asked me to drive back alone while they discussed what to do on their way back.

Man, did I feel left out and felt that they were all talking about my future plan without my input. When they got back, they had decided not to get the money for CADRA but give me a job working for the city and the jail, and they would pay me twenty-five thousand dollars, and I could do my program in the jail but work for the city. I took on this position met, with criminal justice department, gave a speech about everyone who deserved a second chance and how God gave us all a second chance. I took God's word and His twelve-step plan He gave me into the jails and was well received and had great participation in the male and female block. We had one block set up as the Christian block where I was able to go in and preach, and the men formed a chorus group and song gospel songs before I preached. I was asked by a Major of the Sheriff department to assist him in starting a program called Second Chance that would help people coming out of jail begin a new start, and I said that it was what CADRA is doing, and that was part of the Mission. He introduced me to this professor from Norfolk State and a psychiatrist and told me that they would be working with him to receive a grant from the Justice Department, and he wanted me to assign my clients that signed up for CADRA to them, and they would be counselling them.

I referred a few, and the clients said they wanted to be a part CADRA where they could get spiritual help and not just talk to a man that didn't know what they were going through. Because I continued to assign the clients to CADRA the major began to lock me out of my appointments and stopped allowing me to enter the jail, and he lied to Council Conly Phillip and told him I was not coming to the jail.

The women blocks wrote over fifty letters requesting that CADRA continue to do drug counseling session in their blocks, but I was relieved of my duties in order for them to get the grant for their program called Second Chance.

A client, whom I had helped get out of jail by given him a job as a manager of my restaurant, Brown's Fried Chicken, was given the position that they had slotted for me as one of the directors of Second Chance, and he told me that the assistant city manager, told him that my problem was that I really thought I could help those people. That statement confirmed to me that they (city) had no desire to help the citizen but get the money to use for the city's benefits.

I was told by one of the aides of Governor Wilder that only nonprofit organizations would be receiving grants because of the city and state's poor results from the use of funds. I was given a thirty-five unit apartment building because the owner, Mrs. Alexander, said that she believed in my program, and over half her tenants were on drugs and couldn't afford the rent, and she knew I could help them, and she was led to give me the building if I could get the funds to open up my rehab center. I immediately contacted my grant writers, and we applied for funds, and because I knew I would need the city's cooperation, I decided to have a talk with the Assistant City Manager, and I informed him about funds allocated to nonprofit program, and he told me he would talk with the mayor and council to get their support, but what he did was to form his own nonprofit and appointed city workers, who lived in Park Place where I was given the building to apply for grants, and had them fight against the rezoning of my building.

I had been approved by the state health department to open up my rehab center but it needed to be in operation for six months to get financial assistant for each client I had. I applied for a multipurpose use permit from zoning and got a six to one approval, and it was put in paper that the only one who came against the permit was a pastor standing in the way of a Christian program.

We then had to get city council approval, and I needed four votes to get it approved. The mayor and Councilman Phillip were in, and we had two pastors on the council, and the Lord led me to go talk with them and pray with them to hear His voice on this matter because CADRA was led by Him, and it was God's vision. Both men told me it was not about God but the citizens they represented. I prayed with them, and one began to weep because he knew I was right, and he would be coming up against people he went to school with that got him elected, and he would think about supporting us.

A few days before the vote, God led me to go to every house in the neighborhood and get a petition signed in favor of the rehab center, and I got over five hundred names in support of us opening up. We had opposition from other names to signatures and found community that felt having a drug center would lower their value on their properties, and they had a petition signed by them with all their tenants' names on it. I presented the one I had, and they matched the names to signature and found out the ones I had were signed by the tenants, and they threw out their paper and voted.

Father Green, Mayor Leaf, Councilman Philips, and Councilman Wright voted in favor of us having the center. The city manager had another plan, which I didn't expect, and that was to have the building inspectors inspect the building according to a multipurpose use, and they came back with cost of $200,000.00 in renovations that needed to be done before opening up. This was a property that already had tenants and was in good condition.

I went to Tidewater Baptism Association and presented God's vision to them and let them known if they had members who had drug problems they could use the center, and I needed twenty of them to support the vision by giving $10,000.00 each, and they said they would vote on it, but I never got back an answer.

The state health department made a visit to my outreach center to qualify me, and support me opening up the in-house rehab, and the day they came by, God showed them the need and reason.

I was being interviewed when a young man came running in the center, screaming, "Mr. Brown, we need you right now. A girl just got overdosed."

I got up and told them I had to go, and they asked could they tag along, and I said yes. I was taken to a drug house and found the girl out cold, and I began to pray for God to bring her out of this situation, and she opened her eyes, and I picked her up, carried her back to the center, and called 911. Paramedics came to carry her to hospital. The man and women were so impressed because the people had so much respect for me that they knew I was there for them. They said they would do all they could do because I was providing a service that was well needed. They said they would be able to contract my services, but I had to be up and running at least six months, and the money would be based on the number of clients allocated and no fees for renovation or construction expenses. I couldn't raise the fund to open up. The city knocked down the building and rezoned the property to residential.

I had a talk with God and told him that "those who were on my board of directors should be doing what I am doing," and the time, I was used, taken away from what He called me to do, and that was to rescue His people from drugs and help them see the light, what He had done for me, he wanted to do for them.

God told me to call a board meeting and confront them with what I had talked to him about and after that leave the rest to Him. I called Councilman Phillip, Attorney Fiveash, and Professor Aday and requested a meeting. Councilman Phillip set up a breakfast meeting and his wife, Betsy, prepare a great meal. She was very nice to me, and she really admired my faith and commitment to carry out God's work in the city.

We met that morning, and I told them how I felt, and I said to Professor Aday that I knew he knows people who could support CADRA because I read someone had just donated millions to him and the College of William and Mary. I said the same to the other two and the comment I got back was from Councilman Phillips was for us to pray about it. He began to pray, and he asked God to protect the city of Norfolk from a storm that was predicted to hit the city with one-hundred-mile wind. He began to talk to Lord about all the city had, built up, and invested in the building. The city had just built a huge mall downtown and two large hotels.

I remember when they set the plans, and Councilman Phillips called me to go with him to pray over the land, and we asked God for favor to complete the task, and He answered the prayer, and it was completed in very short time. He reminded God that Norfolk is surrounded by water, and a flood will destroy the city. I was waiting on him to ask God about the question of what they should do about getting funds for CADRA because that is what we were suppose to be praying about. He did not mention CADRA at all in his prayer because his concerns were only for the city structures and on the storm.

CADRA was trying to save people in the city who are addicted to drugs. I prayed early that morning and asked God give me sign from Him that I could use to assure them that the vision was from Him, and that I divinely heard from Him.

When Councilman Phillips finish his prayer the Lord whispered to me to tell him, He will answer his prayer and also tell them that the headline in newspaper will *read* "Christians Pray and Turn Back the Storm."

The paper had a picture of the eye of the storm rise up in the sea, looking at the city, and then turned around and went back out to sea. It also stated that Pat Robertson and Christians prayed and turned back the storm. I called them all and asked if they did read the paper, and I told them I knew the vision God gave, which must be done, and I needed to know what was their next move, if it would be about getting the finance to complete the vision.

I received a letter from a CADRA's registered agent that all three had stepped down as board members, and I needed to assign others as board member. The only reason that I could come up with for them quitting is that CADRA was too spiritual for them. As president, secretary, treasurer, and the sole director, we were still able to keep our 501c3 status. I named three of my staff as directors, and I waited on God for the next move because that was the instruction He gave me before the final meeting. I pray you received a blessing from reading this book and get good directions from God to fulfil your purpose.

341 W. Chickasaw RoadTo
Va. Beach, Virginia 23462
August 1, 1999

To Whom It May Concern:

1 am writing this letter to share with you how God has used a man that I have
known for over 50 years. I am Deacon Raymond H. Norman, Sr. of The Mount
Gilead Missionary Baptist Church. I have known Rev. Cleveland Brown and his
family through the years. However, I got to meet Rev. Brown's Spiritual side when
I was asked to meet with him about a "March For Jesus" that he was trying to do
in 1987.

At that time I was the Superintendent of Recreation for the City of Norfolk, Va. My
supervisor informed me to meet with Rev. Brown to see how we could arrange the
"March" by hosting it at the Northside Park in Norfolk.

In talking with Rev. Brown he explained to me how God had given him this vision
(Dec. 1986) to pull the Churches together to begin a "March" through the City to
prepare for Jesus Return.

I have seen him year after year put together this vision that God gave him and I now
realize not only did God speak to him, but to others all over the world about "The
March For Jesus". He kept the faith and pressed on to see God's Vision come true
to the City of Norfolk, Virginia. That same Love for God has raised him up to be an
Anointed Man of God willing to serve all man kind.

I know the "March For Jesus" is not a man's ideal, but one sent from God. I
sincerely urge all Christians to get involve in this mighty move of our God. I know
that God can use anyone if you are willing to be obedient and persistent in carrying
out God's Mission.

I am truly thankful to God that I was able to share in this Vision before it really
became a reality, because it allowed me to see that God has no big people. He will
use those that he see fit to use and not according to man's expectations but his own
will.

Please, get involved with "The March For Jesus", it is the Will of God. I am looking
forward to see you at the next "March For Jesus".

Yours in Christ,

Raymond H. Norman, Sr.
Deacon
Mt. Gilead Baptist Church

114

City of Norfolk
Virginia

Proclamation

WHEREAS, the Norfolk March for Jesus Celebration began in 1990 under the leadership of the Reverend Cleveland Brown and the Community Against Drug Related Activities; and

WHEREAS, Saturday, May 22, 1999 is the ninth annual March for Jesus Celebration in the City of Norfolk, and the theme of this year's march is "Love One Another"; and

WHEREAS, the March for Jesus is now a Hampton Roads regional celebration as well as spreading throughout America and twenty-two countries worldwide; and

WHEREAS, the purpose of the celebration is to encourage brotherly and sisterly love among people of all races, cultures, and denominations;

WHEREAS, the March for Jesus reminds us that strong values and religious teachings are effective solutions to the problems facing our cities.

NOW, THEREFORE, I, PAUL D. FRAIM, Mayor of the City of Norfolk, do hereby proclaim Saturday, May 22, 1999 as

LOVE ONE ANOTHER DAY

in the city of Norfolk, and call upon all citizens to join in this celebration as we recognize that religious teachings, strong values, and loving one another add significantly to the quality of the life of citizens in our City as well as throughout the region.

Given under my hand this 18th day of May 1999.

PAUL D. FRAIM, MAYOR

About the Author

In March of 1990, CADRA (community against drug-related activities) was formed by Rev. Dr. Cleveland Brown in response to the plight of those afflicted with the spiritual and physical bondage caused by drug addiction. Most importantly, it should be noted that CADRA represents a vision given to Rev. Cleveland Brown, for it serves as an alternative, community-based service delivery system, which incorporates a Bible's twelve-step rehabilitation treatment program with a holistic, spiritual approach that results in the total restoration of the mind, body, and spirit of the client. My purpose on earth is to live a life that is pleasing to God, to help all I can on God's earth, to live, and then to find the true purpose that God brought them into this world so they can reach their highest potential and be able to serve their fellowman. God has given us each a purpose on earth that we can serve Him and one another, and our gifts are to be used to help build His kingdom on earth as it is in heaven. I believe the words of God written in the Bible is the thought and will of God that we may have the knowledge of our history, our creation, the creator, and His divine power that will guide us right now and show how to live in this world and prepare us to live in his kingdom.

CPSIA information can be obtained
at www.ICGtesting.com
Printed in the USA
BVHW031820230921
617419BV00001B/8